Playing for Singers

The Mike Greensill Method

A Practical guide to the art of vocal accompaniment for the jazz or cabaret piano player.

Including tips on arranging, chart writing and rehearsal techniques.

Sher Music Co.

©2013 Sher Music Co.
P.O.Box, 445, Petaluma, CA
shermusic.com

TABLE OF CONTENTS

INTRODUCTION

Music schools and conservatories are very good at graduating wonderful jazz pianists who are then thrust, unsuspectingly, into the professional music world hoping to be the next Bill Evans or Herbie Hancock. Little do they realize that they may spend much of their careers accompanying [1]*girl singers*.

Vocal accompaniment is a skill quite different from that of the jazz soloist, but this art is rarely part of a jazz school's curriculum. The purpose of this book is to provide essential and practical knowledge on the art of accompanying singers. It's aimed at everyone, from the beginning student accompanist, to the music teacher, to the professional piano player. In fact, it's for anyone wanting to brush up their skills for the next gig with a vocalist. The book does presume a basic knowledge of jazz harmony and keyboard technique.

One of the most powerful musical marriages of the 20th century is the one between jazz and the [2]*Great American Songbook*, and this repertoire will be the basis for our exploration into the mysteries of the accompanying art. These songs, often from obscure and long forgotten musicals, are kept alive by the jazz musician, the indefatigable [3]*song sleuth* (I plead guilty), and the adventurous vocal artist searching to expand their repertoire. The main reason that so many [4]*standards* are still alive and thriving today is because they are treasured by improvising jazz musicians who delight in their melodic and harmonic magic, and the vocal artists who revel in their witty and intelligent lyrics. This book is aimed at the jazz-influenced piano player but also takes into account the tradition of the theater and cabaret accompanist.

The magic of these standards is that they can be performed in a myriad of styles, from swinging jazz to exotic Latin rhythms, in addition to their original theatrical treatment. There's much to be learned from all the various styles of popular music: keeping in mind that, however you decide to interpret a particular song, the final goal is to create beautiful music and make the singer sound good!

We'll study the obvious, but often forgotten, fundamentals of this art of playing for singers as well as exploring the more subtle and complex tricks of the trade. Whenever the word singer or vocalist appear in this book, you can often substitute the word instrumentalist because many of the same principles apply whether backing a [5]*cabaret* artist or some hot alto player. Though, as we shall discover later, there are also some vital differences.

We'll look at the challenges of accompaniment from the point of view of the solo pianist, the piano/bass duo and the piano trio.

We'll discover all the harmonic options that are best suited to the art of the accompanist and reveal the mysteries of correct voicing or, as I like to think of it, how to sound like an orchestra while playing only 3 notes.

We'll explore the secrets of 'out of tempo' accompaniment, a musical device of some mystery, usually notated as *colla voce*, rubato or freely.

We'll look at the basics of arranging. Accompanists will often find themselves in the role of musical arranger/musical director, and the ability to quickly whip up a professional, easy-to-read chart is an essential skill.

We'll find out how to run a rehearsal, organize a show, and how to conduct from the piano with no hands! We'll deal with the difficult but essential role of accompanist as both diplomat and psychologist.

> *"The best way to make a singer comfortable is to play well for them; make them feel comfortable musically. And then if things get tough - if someone gets stressed out, count to ten... and work it out. It's just music."*
> **Bill Charlap**

Along the way, we'll *learn from the masters*. I've included words of wisdom and personal tips from such great accompanists as Tommy Flanagan, Norman Simmons, Lee Musiker, Jimmy Rowles, Bill Charlap, Mike Renzi, Tedd Firth, Christian Jacob, Sir Richard Rodney Bennett and many others, as well as insights from those singers who play piano for themselves, a particular breed that need to be closely monitored by us keyboard accompanists; singers such as Shirley Horn, Diana Krall and Nat 'King' Cole.

At this point, I need to introduce you to my wife and musical partner, Wesla Whitfield, an extraordinary vocalist with whom I've made 21 albums. It's her guidance, good taste, showbiz savvy and love of the American Songbook that has shaped my career as an accompanist. She'll be featured often in this book because she taught me everything I know about song interpretation and therefore, how to accompany singers!

Some of the best lessons I have ever received on the art of accompanying and playing jazz have been in informal situations rather than the classroom. I studied at Leeds College of Music in England—don't ask how long ago—and often found that I had more fruitful discussions on the finer points of music over a lunchtime pint with my tutors than I ever did in the tutor's study! I have also been able to absorb the knowledge and good taste of my elders and my peers in numerous [7]*green room* conversations over the years.

There's something about jazz that demands that we learn it organically, 'on the streets' so to speak. And so I've tried, along with some feeble attempts at colloquial humor, to make this book sound more like a couple of hipsters chatting on the pavement outside a jazz club than the somber tone of the text book that it really is!

"Accompanying someone cannot be explained by a singer to a pianist. He either knows what to do or he doesn't. An accompanist and a guy who can play the piano are two different things. You have to find someone who is completely sympathetic to the soloist as a singer and not to the soloist as an instrumentalist. It's a completely different thing. Even if a guy can play his buns off, it does not necessarily mean he can accompany a singer. There are some guys who can accompany a singer and who can't play a damn as far as soloing is concerned. That's the difference, and it's a vast difference. A guy must really love to do it. He cannot do it just because he has nothing else to do."
Carmen McCrae - jazz vocalist extraordinaire

Even though I have the greatest respect for Carmen's opinions (she is my favorite jazz singer), I *am* going to risk being foolish and attempt to guide and teach you in the unexplainable and mysterious art of vocal accompaniment. When I started out playing jazz, I couldn't solo or accompany, or play the piano (I was a clarinetist). . .so there's much hope for all of us! Let's dig in.

GLOSSARY

1. Girl singer - Well-respected vocal artist. Also known, irreverently, as a "chick singer."

2. Great American Songbook - A rather pretentious description of the body of popular and Broadway songs written between approximately 1910 and 1970, or as my wife Wesla likes to say, "What happened right after Brahms and right before Buddy Holly."

3. Song Sleuth - Someone who searches the bowels of book stores for obscure sheet music in order to resurrect long-forgotten gems of American melody.

4. Standard - see number 2, above.

5. Cabaret - Cabaret artists can run the gamut from the exotic dancer to the off-duty Broadway star. Generally though, cabaret is thought of as the art of performing songs in an intimate nightclub environment.

6. Colla Voce - is an Italian term, and my music dictionary describes it thus, "With the voice: implying that the accompanist must accomodate and take the time from the singer." *Colla Voce,* in most arrangements, is applied to the verse of the song, although the approach can also work just as well in the body of the tune. Today's singers are aware, more than ever, that great melodic and lyric writing is contained in the verses of these songs and that sometimes the best way to perform the verses is in a conventional manner; a style that demands a close rapport between vocalist and piano player. I love verses. They often seem like miniature art songs, and there's much opportunity for harmonic experimentation. I caution not to experiment too much, however, the reasons for which I'll explain in a later chapter. The integrity of the song and the singer's intended interpretation must always come first.

7. Green Room - A place where musicians/performers, especially in formal concert settings, hang out before going on stage. The specific origin of the term is lost to history, which has led to many imaginative theories and claims. One story is that London's Blackfriars Theater (1599) included a room behind the scenes; this room happened to be painted green. Here the actors waited to go on stage, and it was called 'the green room.' Some English theaters contained several green rooms, each ranked according to the status and the salary of the actor. One could be fined for using a green room above one's station. Jazz musicians should be so lucky to play anywhere with multiple green rooms!

CHAPTER 1

The Basics

THE FOUR RULES: 1. Listen, 2. Listen, 3. Listen, and then finally, number 4. Listen! This cannot be said too often. The success of all musical performances depends on the ability to make music together. The only way to do that is to listen closely to the other musicians, and yes—all joking aside—the singer is one of the musicians.

Of course making great music requires use of the most important musical instrument you possess; your brain. Think about the songs. Think about what you will play. Think about how little you'll need to play. Think about the lyrics. Think about the vocalist's natural style and how it can be best showcased. Think about how to organize a rehearsal. And most of all, think about how to "make music". The beauty of using your brain as a musical instrument is its portability! All of the above can be done while stuck in traffic! I find that I can rehearse accompanying strategies, fingerings and difficult passages away from the piano by imagining playing them.

The first opportunity to listen closely is in rehearsal. This is the time to listen very closely to the vocalist's natural phrasing and decide on [8]*comping* strategies. A word about comping: Comping is generally understood to be the rhythmic placement of chords underneath the vocal line. It requires instant decisions about where to place chords and how long to sustain them—all of which is based on the vocalist's phrasing. Great comping will provide the vocalist with a rhythmic and harmonic carpet, whereas busy and inappropriate "comping" can be a distraction. "Less is more" is always the accompanist's mantra. I recently read a critique of this old adage that said: with 'less is more' all you end up with is less! But this doesn't apply to us. In the case of the accompanist, less really is more. The art of comping is covered in depth in Chapter 4.

Basic Tenets of the Accompanist's Art

1. TEMPO - In rehearsal, listen closely to the singer's needs in terms of the tempo and rhythmic approach. Piano players can be very strong willed and opinionated, but important artistic decisions like tempo should be made by the vocalist. Don't just set a tempo thinking that you know best. This will not endear you to the vocalist. Sometimes a singer doesn't have a strong opinion on tempo, and that's when one can be more assertive. There may be clues to tempo and rhythmic feel in the arrangements, but that's

not always the case. You may, of course, believe that your tempo is the best artistically, and this is when your essential diplomatic skills should kick in. Believe me, all these tricks of the trade have been learned through bitter experience!

Memorize the right tempo for a tune so you can recreate it easily on the gig. I have an electronic metronome that I find indispensable. It has a silent flashing red light to indicate tempos, and so it can be subtly referred to between tunes and that's saved me many times on gigs with very little rehearsal.

If you're in charge of tempos on the gig, learn to count tempos clearly. There's nothing worse than musicians snapping their fingers and expecting you to automatically know where [9]*one* is. If you're playing for the more formal cabaret/theatrical show, you can ensure seamless transitions by making accurate notes on tempos during rehearsal. You will also need to note where [10]*segues* and/or [11]*patter* occur. However, there are times, especially with jazz singers, when the vocalist will want to be in complete charge of setting song tempos.

2. CHARTS & KEYS - Hopefully the singers you accompany will have decent charts. But depending on the stage of your career - are you playing at Carnegie Hall or your local saloon - you'll find yourself reading [12]*charts* that vary in quality from the sublime to the ridiculous. Charts can run the gamut from a professionally copied Johnny Mandel score, to [13]*chicken scratches* from the local society pianist, to no charts at all. These days it seems that everyone, including me, write charts on the computer. These charts can often be as bad as the chicken scratches because few arrangers have spent enough time mastering the notation programs. Check out Chapter 5 on arranging where we delve into the art of chart writing.

You'll need to be able to think fast on your feet in rehearsal, ask questions of the singer and make lots of notes. Often the most confusing area of sight reading new charts involves the [14]*map reading*. Most [15]*train wreck*s happen when a musician finds himself asking: "Where the hell do I go next?". Rehearsal is the time to make sure that the road map is clear and understood. When we get to the chapter on arranging, I'll cover this subject more thoroughly.

It really helps to be good at transposition, and it is especially useful when one is in rehearsal and going over new or prospective songs with a vocalist. Of course the difficulty of this task depends somewhat on the style of music being played. For example, it's much easier to transpose a standard from F to B flat when reading a basic lead sheet consisting of melody and chords as compared to playing a Broadway show tune where you might be expected to play the accompaniment exactly as written and up a fourth!

Accompanists are expected to play in all keys. Therefore practicing in all keys is a must. Obviously some keys are harder to play than others, but they will come up from time to time. But sometimes difficult keys are unavoidable. My wife, the vocalist Wesla Whitfield, sings "I've Got The World On A String" in B. We chose that key based on the belt note she wanted to sing at the end of the song and that belt note was best in the key of C. But, we also wanted a key change, so that meant starting off in the key of B so we could end up in C! Playing in these keys is a challenge unique to the vocal accompanist because rarely does the saxophone player turn to you and call "All The Things You Are" in B.

> *There is an apocryphal story concerning vocalist Anita O'Day, who was known to call for songs in B major. Eventually one of her pianists discovered that she didn't have perfect pitch, and it was quite all right to play them in B flat! She never complained.*

3. PHRASING - Listen closely to the singer's phrasing. This will give you important clues as to your chord placement, especially in out-of-tempo passages. Some singers will phrase the same way every time, and others will almost never repeat themselves. I often watch the singer's mouth in order to discover where breaths are being taken so I can know when a phrase is about to begin or end, giving me many clues as to placement of the chords and even where to use a tasty [16]*fill*. In 'out of tempo' passages a singer may prefer a chord to sound before starting a phrase, or they may be confident enough with their pitch to let you sound the chord at the same time as their entrance. These musical tactics should be ironed out in rehearsal. Of course every musical circumstance is different, making it difficult to give hard and fast rules. Listen, listen, is our mantra.

4. LISTEN TO YOURSELF - Ask yourself, 'am I playing too much? Am I playing these notes just because they sound good to me, or are they in fact adding to the singer's performance?' There is a lovely [17]*Jimmy Rowles* story on this very subject. It happened while he was playing for singer Sarah Vaughn. Receiving accolades at intermission, a fan said, "You played so beautifully, I didn't know whether to listen to you or Sarah." Jimmy realized he'd been playing 'too pretty' because the listener was distracted from Sarah who was, after all, supposed to be the focal point of the performance.

5. LESS IS ALWAYS MORE - This is where it helps to be less than a virtuoso. I don't have a lot of technique, and so I'm not in any danger of playing [18]*Art Tatum* type runs during a vocalist's sensitive performance of a sparse ballad—though God knows I've often heard that sort of excess coming from otherwise wonderful musicians. Jimmy Rowles also said, "Think of what to play, then play half of it."

6. DON'T PLAY THE MELODY - It seems an obvious error, but one often hears the melody being played as part of the accompaniment. This is rarely heard in the jazz world, but in the Broadway theater tradition, the melody is often played in the orchestral accompaniment. Consequently the singer is forced to phrase exactly as written in the score. In most creative situations a singer will not want to hear the melody because it will interfere with their own ideas for phrasing. And unless you're doing it on purpose, we don't want to hear any unison line with the vocal.

I used to think that this rule also applied to the way one should voice a chord, i.e. don't put the melody note at the top of a chord. But there are many exceptions to this rule and many circumstances with exotic chords where it's very desirable to have the melody note on top of the chord. It's situations like these where the skills of arranger and accompanist often merge.

> *"When you're subbing for another accompanist, the singer's comfort and support eclipses the accompanist's ego of wanting his individual voice to be heard. Our excellence is going to a gig and being a copy cat and fitting in, and that's an excellence in itself, even though we're not presenting our individual voice. It's something highly professional, a craftsman of the highest order."*
> **Lee Musiker**

For example; in a recent arrangement for a San Francisco vocalist, I was lazy and I wrote out only the chord names for a passage I'd re-harmonized in "The Nearness Of You" instead of providing more comprehensive information. The singer took the chart to an open mike with a very competent piano player, and the arrangement worked well except for this one passage of [19]*alternate harmony* I'd thrown in. I realize now, the harmony needed to be spelled out in full to be played properly. On the following page is Hoagy Carmichael's wonderful tune as it appears in the published sheet music.

Example 1a

Example 1b   And here's what I'd originally written in the singer's chart.....

Example 1c   But this is what I should have written, in order to give the pianist
enough information to voice the accompanying chords correctly.

This example illustrates the frequent need for the accompanist to assume the multiple
roles of arranger, musical director and conductor, even if not formally assigned these
roles. All these skills are required to be the complete accompanist, and we'll explore

them in chapter 6.

7. CHORD VOICINGS

Music needs air and space, and uncluttered chord voicing is therefore essential. Amazingly, with just the right two or three notes in the chords, the piano can sound like a full orchestra. Too many notes in the chord can result in muddy voicing. I delve into the details of more complex harmonic voicing in chapter 4.

8. LEARN THE LYRICS AND MELODIES

Make it your business to learn the lyrics and melodies to songs when working with singers. From a practical standpoint it can be a lifesaver should they forget the lyrics. You don't have to be line perfect, but you'll be amazed at how much information seeps into the brain and how useful that can be for your own phrasing if you keep the lyrics in mind. Knowing the intent of the lyric will enable you, in your accompaniment, to paint appropriate "musical pictures" of what is being lyrically described; the sea, a bird, a bright golden haze on the meadow, twelve o'clock tales, etc. In the immortal words of Lester Young, 'you have to learn the words in order to be able to play the song properly', though what he actually said was, "Ya gotta know the lyric,[20]*lady*."

"Pianists who love working with singers and are comfortable being accompanists have one common denominator; they all love songs. There's no question that, besides appreciating and being in love with the structure of how the songs are built just purely on a musical level, they love the other key element; the lyricist! So often when instrumentalists are learning these songs they're learning only half of them by learning 50%, which is just the music. "
Bill Charlap

"I actually like to have the melody note, the soprano note, in my pinkie. It makes your support solid because, and I learned this from Tony (Bennett), you don't want to voice above the melody."
Lee Musiker
(pianist for Tony Bennett, Barbara Cook, Maureen McGovern, Mark Murphy)

GLOSSARY

1. Comping - The rhythmic placement of accompanying chord patterns.

2. One - First beat of the bar.

3. Segue - In music, segue is a direction to the performer. It means continue (to the next section) without a pause. It comes from the Italian "it follows". In the jazz world, it usually means 'go on' to the next tune, either under the applause of the previous tune, or at least continuing without any interruption for 'patter'.

4. Patter - Amusing 'nightclub style' dialogue for use between musical selections. (See also Chapter 6 - putting together a show)

5. Charts - Interchangeable with arrangement, but I tend to think of the chart as the physical piece of paper that has the music written on it and the arrangement as the actual imagining of the accompaniment of the song.

6. Chicken Scratches - Unreadable hand-written charts.

7. Map Reading - Interpreting the road map of the chart. e.g. checking where the repeats occur, when to take the coda, etc.

8. Train Wreck - When the music falls apart and comes to a stop, often when someone mis-interprets the road map.

9. Fill - An instrumental melodic interlude played between a singers phrases, or under a sustained vocal note.

10. Jimmy Rowles - Legendary Los Angeles jazz pianist, wit and accompanist. Played for Billie Holiday, Sarah Vaughn, Peggy Lee, Carmen McCrae and many others.

11. Art Tatum - Jazz piano god, with technique to spare.

12. Alternate Harmony - Harmony that's different, and often more exotic, than the written sheet music changes.

13. Lady - Lester Young called everybody 'lady.'

CHAPTER 2

Solo Piano - Vocal Accompaniment

Due to either artistic decisions or, more often, financial constraints, the piano accompanist will often find themselves on many gigs where it's "just the two of us," you and the vocalist. In this chapter we'll explore how to accompany a vocalist without the aid of any musical safety nets!

The magic of the piano is that it is the complete instrument. It can be the whole orchestra. That means you're able to provide harmony, rhythm and melody all at the same time. Wow, that's power. But just because you're the whole orchestra doesn't mean that you have to play [21]*World War 3* behind the unsuspecting singer. "Less is more" is our mantra, along with the aforementioned listen, listen, listen. But why is less, more? Well, for a start we have to remember why we're here. Our job is to showcase the singer and the song and not to upstage them! And sometimes silence can be a beautiful and dramatic musical tool. In fact, I've found that the hardest thing to do in accompanying is to edit yourself. But with that in mind, we do have to keep a lot of balls in the air at one time. We have to provide the correct harmonic carpet for the singer to float over, and we have to provide the appropriate rhythmic pulse. Obviously there will be situations where a more vigorous accompaniment will be needed in order to provide the right effect (e.g., in Latin rhythms and modern pop songs).

Part 1 - The Vocalist's Starting Note

I'm going to start with something that may seem obvious but often is not well thought-out by the accompanist—how to give a singer their starting note, whether a ballad or a swinger. I didn't realized this was a problem until I started hearing complaints from singers working with young piano players who seemed to have no idea how this basic need was accomplished.

And unless you're dealing with a very talented, adventurous and experienced singer, we don't need to hear excerpts from the Schoenberg-influenced concerto you've written, and been using as a 4 bar intro to "Satin Doll." Simplicity is our watchword.

The first thing to take into account is not only the identity of the starting note but what harmonic area that note inhabits. For example, the ballad "Young and Foolish" in the key of C starts on G, the fifth of the tonic chord. The melody of "Honeysuckle Rose" also begins on the fifth of the scale but has harmony that starts on the ii chord, Dm7 in the key of C. So even though the accompanist is attempting to give the vocalist a clue to the same starting note (G) the approach needs to be quite different.

Example 1a. Here's a simple "out-of-tempo" introduction for a melody starting on the fifth of the tonic chord using the wonderful aforementioned ballad, "Young and Foolish."

Note the use of a "bell tone" on the 4th beat of bar 1. Bell tones are a useful and musical way of reinforcing the singers note without being too pedantic about it!

Example 1b. The melody in this example again starts on the fifth of the scale but the first chord of the tune is now a ii chord. This example is "Honeysuckle Rose" in the key of C, and the first chord is Dm11.

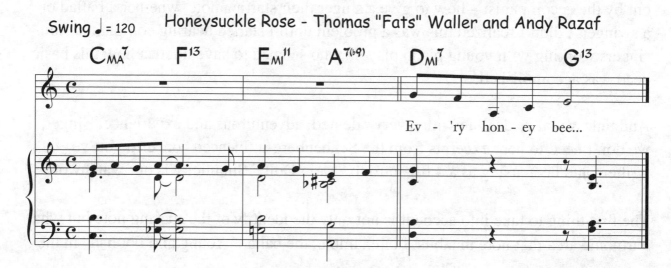

Notice that the melody line on beats 3 and 4 in bar 2 also leads the singer to the correct starting note. This is known as [22]*voice leading*.

Example 1c. When playing an intro to a song in a minor key, it's essential to give the singer a clue to that tonality. In bar 2 of this example, we've done that by flattening the fifth of the ii chord, making it Dm7b5 and raising the fifth of the V chord making it G7+. As a bonus, our melodic line (bar 2, beat 3) utilizes the sharpened 9th and the flattened 9th of the G7 dominant chord, and again the voice leading gently guides the singer to the starting note. And there's no doubt that we're in Cm!

You and the Night and the Music - Howard Dietz and Arthur Schwartz

Example 1d. One of the most difficult starting notes for a vocalist to hear is the melody that starts on the 3rd of the scale in a minor key. "How Deep is the Ocean" or the verse to "More Than You Know" are great examples. Here again we use altered chords to set up the tonality but we make sure that our melodic voice leading leads (so to speak) the singer to the correct starting note. BTW, I'm setting a lot of these examples in a typical "girl singer's" key because that's what you'll most often be faced with. Here's the start of the verse of "More Than You Know," (following page).

As an aside, in all of the musical examples, I've written the chord symbols as you might see them on a lead sheet. But, in these examples, I've often voiced the chords with notes not actually described in the chord symbols. e.g. in bar 2 of the above example I've added an "A" to the Gm chord, coloring it in a personal way, while, of course, making sure that it's appropriate to the vocal line.

> *"Though introductions are often improvised, sometimes the vocalist is most comfortable with the same arranged intro each time. Stacey Kent favored hearing the same intro for "What Are You Doing The Rest Of Your Life," which has a challenging opening vocal line that starts on the 3rd of the scale in a minor key."*
> **David Newton** (pianist for Stacey Kent)

If you have any doubts as to the best way to give the vocalist a clue to the starting note of the song, a good idea is to play the last 4 or 8 bars of the melody as an intro. However, there is a large group of people (count me among them) who dislike telegraphing the tune to the audience by quoting from the melody as an introduction. But if you're in a situation where you're not sure of the singer's ability, it's better to be safe than sorry.

An example of a tune where an appropriate ad lib intro is sometimes difficult to invent is "Autumn Leaves." It's in E minor and the melody pick-up starts on E but the first chord is Am7 which is the ii chord of the relative major key of G. So if you treat the song as being in Em and inadvertently end your intro on the dominant of Em which is B7 (usually a logical choice), the singer isn't going to have a clue how to come in. But by playing the last 4 bars of the tune, there will be no doubt as to the starting note of the vocalist's pick-up.

Example 1e.   If, like me and a lot of singers, you don't want to telegraph the melody of the song in the introduction, utilize the harmony of the last 4 bars of the song and invent a new melody over those changes. Even better, make that melody a paraphrase of the original tune. Here are the last 4 bars of "Autumn Leaves", followed by a paraphrased intro.

Autumn Leaves - Joseph Kosma/Johnny Mercer/Jaques Prevert

But I miss you most of all my dar-ling, when au-tumn leaves start to fall.

The fall-ing

All these examples are basic 'middle of the keyboard' introductions for all you beginners. But don't forget, as you progress, that you are in command of a piano, an instrument with great range and feeling. Many of the accompanists I interviewed talked about thinking orchestrally when playing—especially when in accompanist mode. So let your imagination flow, think of your melodic line as a flute solo with 4 French Horns playing the harmonic accompaniment. Or, as in example 1e ("Autumn Leaves"), you could think. . . oboe solo with the violas, cellos and basses playing the harmony.

Thinking orchestrally will also help make your melodic lines *sing*[23] and separate them from the accompaniment. The ability to lyrically bring out a melody line is an essential part of being a good piano player. Try playing the melody line of Example 1e on its own. Play it as legato as possible. Take advantage of the piano's [24]*escape mechanism* by keeping your fingers close to the keys when you go from note to note. It's also important for your [25]*touch* on the piano to have nuance (i.e., get your melodic line to have more heft and brilliance than your accompanying chords).

Now that the singer has his/her starting note let's look at how we might approach solo accompanying in terms of the tempos we'll encounter from ballad to up-tempo. We'll deal with "out-of-tempo" solo playing in chapter 4.

Part 2 - Ballad Accompaniment

On the surface, ballad accompaniment might seem the easiest. After all we're playing slowly! But because of the slow tempo, we might be inclined to fill every available space with notes—not always a good idea. We mustn't underestimate the dramatic power of silence in ballad accompaniment. Ballad playing, in fact, might require us to do the most editing of ideas in all of our playing.

It may seem that in harping on about silence and editing I'm trying to stifle your creativity and ability to add to the excitement of the performance, but I mean nothing of the sort. Each situation is different. There are singers who like their pianists to be equal partners (usually of the modern jazz singer school—pianist Christian Jacob and vocalist Tierney Sutton are a wonderful example) and there are singers who want the accompanist to be heard and not seen (often the more traditional style of singer *a la* Peggy Lee or Doris Day, and not so much in fashion these days—more is the pity). But I feel that the minimalist approach is the best place for the beginner to start. I think it is important to strip down our ideas and really think about each note we intend to play. It's easy to add licks to our performance, but hard to take them away. And remember that the singer's ability to tell the story is paramount.

Keeping all of the aforementioned in mind, we're now ready to go on with this great ballad performance. Even though the tempo is slow, your ^{26}time is of the utmost importance. Slow is hard. It's easy to speed up, and sometimes by the time you've finished your solo and the singer has returned, the tempo is at 90 b.p.m. instead of the 60 b.p.m. where it started! Remember, we're playing solo, and there's no drummer to yell at us. We're on our own. In this situation, the main thing to remember is to relax. Don't let those wrists seize up. When he found himself getting tense, the great Jimmy Rowles would literally take his hand off the keyboard, let his arm hang down, and shake it out.

Ballad accompaniment can be as simple as just playing the chord changes on the beats where they occur. Here's an example of that style on the lovely standard "When I Fall In Love."

Example 2a.

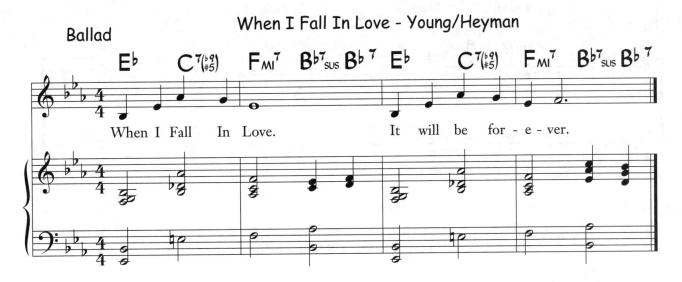

Note that on the 3rd and 4th beats of bars 2 and 4, we employ some movement in the right hand to avoid stagnating the time.

> *As an aside, Lee Musiker, (Tony Bennett's wonderful music director), told*
> *me that because so much of accompanying consists of laying down chords,*
> *he makes sure to practice his scales and arpeggios every day in order to*
> *keep his finger technique in great shape. Good advice!*

In fact, it's often good to play all 4 beats in the bar. But unlike rock and pop piano styles where the comping usually consists of the repetition of the same simple chord voicing, in the same register, for beats on end, we want to have a more varied, sophisticated, approach. In example 2b, on the next page, the first two beats in the right hand are identical voicing but I've changed the register by an octave. I've used octave inserts on beat 4 of bar 1, and beat 2 of bar 2 and 3. This allows the accompaniment to breath while still stating all 4 beats in the bar.

Example 2b

Ballad

When I Fall In Love - Young/Heyman

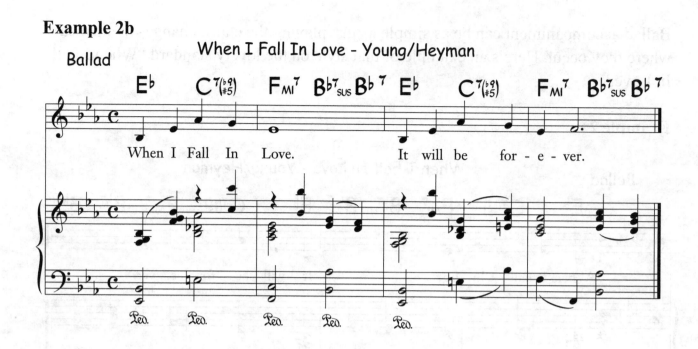

Diversion - Some Thoughts On Pedal Technique

Let's talk a bit about pedal technique. In the previous example you'll notice there are pedal markings under the bass clef. Playing in this ballad style demands very subtle use of the [27]*sustain pedal.* On the first two beats, I use the pedal just to the end of the first beat in order to move my right hand and get to the second beat in a smooth way. Musically this is described as "off on 2." But on the second and third beats, I'll hold the pedal for the full two beats. This is because the octave C on the 4th beat is more of an accent than a new harmonic thought. And so, even though the sustain pedal is depressed, it won't sound muddy, which can happen if you allow two different chords to run into each other with the sustain depressed. This sort of subtle use of the sustain pedal will enable you to have the [28]*legato* sound that is essential for smooth ballad playing and yet have a secure and succinct time feel. The thing to remember about the sustain pedal is that when pressed down, it sustains all the strings on the piano by moving all the dampers away from the strings and allowing them to vibrate freely. Therefore, all notes played will continue to sound until the pedal is released. Using the sustain pedal also causes all the strings to vibrate sympathetically, which enriches the piano's tone, but as I said, you have to be very careful not to make sustained passages sound muddy. The skilled use of the sustain pedal is essential to solo accompanying. There's nothing worse, or amateurish, than too much pedal!

While we're at it, let's not ignore the [29]*soft pedal* (or *una corda* pedal). I tend to use it to a fault for many reasons. As an accompanist, I'm always concerned about not swamping the singer in sound, and having an efficient way to lower the volume is always good. Remember that on a grand piano, this pedal shifts the whole action, including the keyboard, slightly to the right. So the hammers which normally strike three strings to sound a note, strike only two of them. This softens the note and also changes its tone quality. On a grand piano all the notes from F an octave and a 5th below middle C, to the very top, have three strings.

When using the soft pedal on a grand piano, tone quality is also affected. This occurs because we've forced the remaining two strings that are being struck to make contact with a part of hammer felt which is not often hit (due to the whole action being shifted). This results in a duller sound, as opposed to the bright sound which is usually produced (due to the felt on the hammer being hardened from over-use). I sometimes like a dull sound when accompanying. After all we're not playing a concerto and trying to cut through the sound of a massive orchestra.

There is another, unintended advantage in using the soft pedal on a grand piano. If the piano is slightly out of tune and some of the unisons aren't perfect, the striking of only two strings can really help mitigate this problem.

On an upright piano the soft pedal operates a mechanism which moves the hammers' resting position closer to the strings. Since the hammers have less distance to travel, this reduces the speed at which they hit the strings, and hence the volume is reduced. But this does not change tone quality, or the number of strings that are struck, in the same way the *una corda* pedal does on a grand piano.

Remember, on the grand piano, the whole action shifts to the right and the hammers strike only two strings of each note. While on the upright, the hammers are moved closer to the strings.

While we're thinking about pedals, let's briefly touch on the *sostenuto* pedal, the middle one on a modern grand piano. This pedal, which I feel is underutilized, especially by me, sustains *only* those notes which are depressed at the same time the pedal is depressed—allowing future notes played to be unaffected by the sustain. This is very useful in Rubato intros where one can sustain a chord and then play a crisp little run above it, as in this next example. You play the chord, apply the *sostenuto* pedal, then play the 16th note run. The chord sustains and the run sparkles without the sounds running into one another.

Example 3

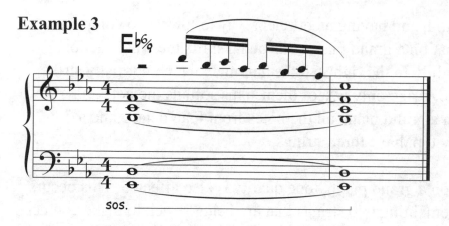

All this discussion of pedals came up because we were trying to play our chordal accompaniment for ballads, smoothly. Sometimes the best way to practice playing legato with the sustain pedal is to start out not using it at all (like an organist who has no sustain, just his finger technique) and then gradually add sustain to the parts that you want to sound legato. It will eventually become second nature.

In our style of playing, it's hard to notate exactly how much one should use the pedal, and so you'll almost never see it notated on commercial charts/lead sheets. Like a lot of accompanying, pedaling is an instinctive art, but that instinct can be nurtured by constant practice and preparation. As Bill Charlap says, "You need a full toolbox." Again, just to hammer (ahem) the point home, there's nothing worse than over-pedaling. It produces a mushy and amorphous sound with all of the the chords running into one another, and it can also muddy up the time feel.

A lot of accompanists these days, as real pianos become scarcer, are forced to play electric pianos. And to me the worst problem with even the very best electrics is the fact that there is no sympathetic vibrations from real strings. It's not a real piano! I have to admit that when I'm in this situation I prefer to just acknowledge that this is a "fake" instrument and utilize the "fake" sounds. I'm partial to the Fender Rhodes setting, phase shifter on!

Ballad Accompaniment (continued)

After that long diversion, let's get back to ballad accompaniment. When playing ballad accompaniment in a jazz style, I much prefer non-rolled, non-arpeggiated chords, (i.e., chords in which all the notes are sounded at the same time). When the chords are rolled, the feel of where the *time* falls is often lost. In some situations, a subtle roll is appropriate, (e.g., chords in the left hand that demand a large stretch). But in general, we jazzers like the chord to occur on beat one and not have the playing of the chord take a beat and a half.

This brings us to a physical observation. How big are your hands? Can you stretch a tenth in your left hand? Some of us can and some of us can't. Some of us can stretch some tenths but not all of them. Some stretches are reasonably easy; C to E; and some are hard; Ab to C. Why would we want this skill? It helps with chord voicing, of course. The larger gap between the bass note and the next note of the chord gives a cleaner, more open sound. It mimics the [30]*overtone series*.

Example 4a - Here's a simple C69 chord.

Example 4b - But here's a way to achieve the same effect with smaller hands.

Example 4c - Or you can play a fifth in the left hand and use the right-hand thumb to play the tenth.

There are pianists who use what are called "walking tenths" in the left hand, and we'll look at that style in the next section on "medium tempo" accompanying.

As for which chords and what voicing's are best to play in all the musical situations that you'll find yourself, there are many great books on jazz harmony—I recommend Mark Levine's wonderful book, "The Jazz Piano Book." A comprehensive study of harmony is beyond the scope of this book. But I will say that an extensive harmonic knowledge is an essential part of the accompanist's art, especially in the areas of transposition and re-harmonization of songs. We will have a brief look at chord voicings, for use when comping, in chapter 3, and a look at re-harmonization of standards in chapter 5 on arranging.

Listening suggestions - *Solo Piano and Vocal*

"Ella Sings Gershwin" - Ella Fitzgerald and Ellis Larkins
"Where is Love" - Irene Kral and Alan Broadbent
"Live at the Dug" - Carmen McCrae (Carmen playing for herself)
"Short Stories" and "Slow Hot Wind" - Janis Siegel and Fred Hersch

Part 3 - Medium-Tempo Accompaniment

Let's deal with rhythm first. When playing solo piano in a jazz context, one of the puzzles we have to solve is how to recreate the feel of a full rhythm section—especially that difference between playing with a 'floaty 2 feel' and 'swinging in 4.' The first thing we need is good 'time.' That, of course, means not only *not* speeding up or slowing down, but providing a steady rhythmic pulse for the listener and the vocalist to hang on to. This feeling of a 'steady pulse' needs to be there, whether you're playing all the beats in a bar, or only some of them.

How does one practice keeping good time? I'm not personally a fan of rehearsing with a metronome as it is almost too rigid and not human, but it does help some people. I found it better to have an apprenticeship with an experienced drummer and bass player. There's nothing like having a drummer throwing sticks at your head when you're rushing the beat to focus the mind. Jazz time can be a sticky proposition, especially when playing solo. When you do play with a rhythm section, there are players who push the beat, play way behind the beat or right on top of it, and yet they can all be said to have 'good time.'

TWO FEEL - This is the one of the trickiest feels to replicate in solo piano accompaniment, because in order to succeed, it requires having complete confidence in your own sense of time and that of the vocalist. With a 'two feel,' we're trying to create that 'floating' feeling we get when a bass is not [31]*walking,* but playing only on beats 1 and 3 with occasional connecting lines. Here's an example of a "2 feel" accompaniment for solo piano on the Ray Noble tune "The Touch Of Your Lips".

The quarter note = 120.

Example 5a

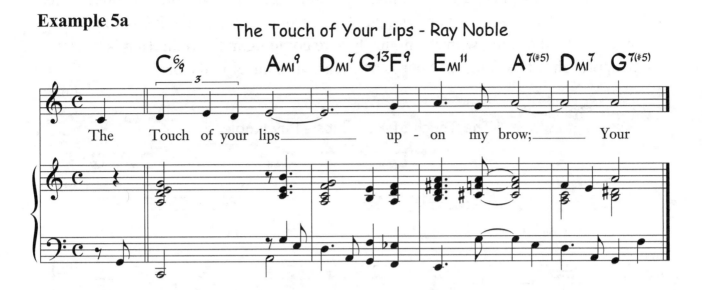

The Touch of Your Lips - Ray Noble

Notice that the right hand is calmer and more sustained while the left is more rhythmic, letting us know where the time is in relation to the melody. One must also remember that a singer may not phrase anything like the above sheet music phrasing, and reacting to that is, of course, the challenge of the jazz accompanist. You have to think on your feet and be ready to change your musical plans according to the phrasing that you're hearing from the singer. Be prepared to change directions in an instant so that you can always support the singer with your harmonic carpet, and yet be prepared to fill in the gaps between phrases, either melodically or rhythmically, wherever they occur to provide musical continuity.

Listening suggestions

The perfect example of how to replicate the *two feel* as a solo piano player can be found on the iconic Bill Evans and Tony Bennett duet CDs. Listen to "When in Rome" and the tune we're using as an example in this chapter, "The Touch of Your Lips."

"The Complete Tony Bennett/Bill Evans Recording
"Message From The Man In The Moon" - Wesla Whitfield and Mike Greensill
"Marian McPartland's Piano Jazz - featuring Shirley Horn" - Fantasy Records

SWING FEEL - The obvious way to recreate a swinging feel "in 4" is to walk a bass line with your left hand. I have to admit not liking this approach too much, as it often sounds to me as if the piano player really wished there *was* a bass player on the gig! We have this vast instrument at our disposal, so we can find other ways to create the propulsive effect of a swinging trio. Though, as with all things artistic, nothing is black and white, and there are many, many exceptions to my own "no bass lines" rule. What we want is a creative mix of walking bass, walking tenths, passing sevenths, etc. in the left hand along with rhythmically sure comping in the right. Here's how we might approach "The Touch of Your Lips" in a swinging "4 in the bar."

Example 5b

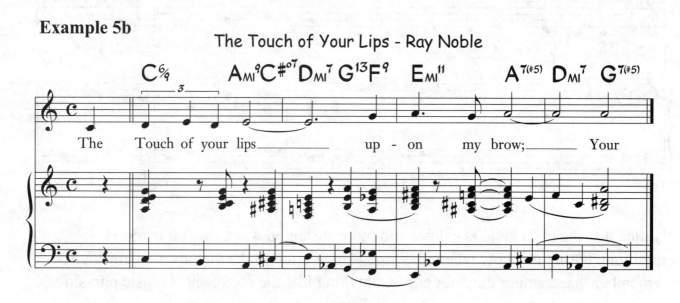

The bass line consists mainly of walking notes with a couple of passing sevenths on beats 3 and 4 of measure 2. The right hand indicates the harmony with rhythmic kicks. It also joins the left hand briefly on the last beat of the 3rd measure to emulate *walking tenths*—which we'll finally look at in detail in the next paragraph. I've also added passing harmony. Note that on the last beat of measure 1, the Am7 becomes C#o, a passing chord, to lead us to the Dm9. This is the sort of invention that we need to come up with in order to make the accompaniment interesting and not repetitive. The passing chords I used are incumbent upon knowing exactly where the melody is at that moment. If the melody over the Am7 in measure 1 had been a C, then I wouldn't have used the C#o passing chord. These are instant decisions that one must make when accompanying, and they point out the importance of either having the melody on the chart in front of you or of already knowing the tune and therefore the amount of harmonic risks one may take. And of course, you need to develop your *ears* so that you can tell exactly what note the vocalist is currently singing!

Walking Tenth's - If you are able to stretch a tenth, then it's worth looking at the principles of the *walking tenth* style. The master and originator of this style was Teddy Wilson, who in the late 1930's was the accompanist on all those great Billie Holiday [32]*sides*. This jazz piano style was a bridge between the [33]*stride piano* style of the 1920's and early thirties and the more sparse, less left-hand heavy, modern approach of the [34]*be-boppers*. This style of accompaniment was later refined and perfected by the wonderful accompanist Ellis Larkins. Ellis was unusual in the jazz world, in that he was almost exclusively an accompanist. As a personal aside, it was Ellis's solo accompanying of Ella Fitzgerald on the wonderful album, "Ella Sings Gershwin" that inspired me and set me on my own career path as an accompanist. This album is essential listening. These days, I think a well-rounded piano player needs to play and understand all styles. Again, in Bill Charlap's words, we need to possess a complete tool box.

The basis of walking tenths is to move in a scale-like fashion, like the first 3 beats in bar one of example 6, mixed in with step-wise movement, like on beats 3 and 4.

Example 6

You'll notice that in bar 2 on beat 2, I've used a passing chord with a more modern voicing. It's a Db9 using just the 3rd, 7th and 9th, very Bill Evans-ish in the context of Teddy Wilson. The 4th beat of bar 2 also uses a passing chord, but this one's a tenth, Gb7. The marvelous thing about walking tenths is that it gives such a sense of forward motion. Here's our standby, "The Touch of Your Lips," using walking tenths. You'll notice that there are some passing sevenths mixed in and, whenever physically possible, as in beats 2 and 3 of the first measure, I also play the seventh of the m7 chords (with my index finger) in the middle of the tenth for an even fuller sound.

Example 7a

The Touch of Your Lips - Ray Noble

Having big hands is nice, but stretching a 10th isn't essential at all, as we've seen. We have many ways to achieve the same effect. Whether it's utilizing the right hand thumb to play the top of the 10th, or rolling the chords, there are numerous tricks to achieve the same sound.

Listening - Swing Feel

"Ella Sings Gershwin" - Ella Fitzgerald with Ellis Larkins on Piano
(I know, I've already recommended this album - but it's important!)
"Jubilee" - Daryl Sherman and Dave McKenna.
"Solo Piano - The Keystone Transcriptions" - Teddy Wilson

The Teddy Wilson listening suggestion is a solo album, *sans* singer, because it so well illustrates his style of playing. You can imagine using all of his left-hand ideas when accompanying a vocalist, and the rest of his playing ain't too shabby either! I include the Dave McKenna album because the great swing pianist makes walking bass lines sound like Bach two-part inventions and in so doing gives a lie to my bass line prejudice. As well as playing great left-hand bass lines, Dave was also very adept at playing "4 in the bar" patterns of chords with his left hand *a la* Erroll Garner. Erroll was, of course, the master of this style, but he didn't do any accompanying of singers. Dave didn't do a lot of vocal accompanying either, but that doesn't mean that you couldn't utilize this style in your accompaniments. It's essential to steal from the best.

Here's an example of the "Garner Style." You'll notice that because the harmony is taken care of in the left hand, the right hand is free to fill in melodically between the singer's phrases. What we're really doing is imitating the rhythm guitar.

Example 7b

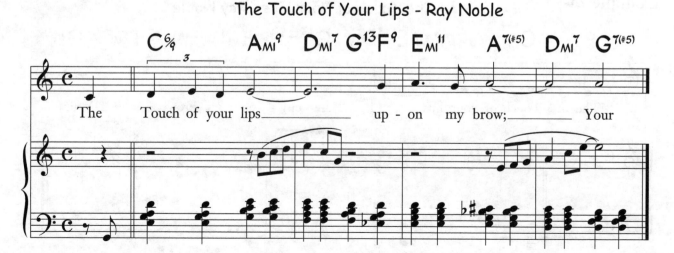

The Touch of Your Lips - Ray Noble

At slow or medium tempos, the left-hand chords are played straight, but at faster tempos the left-hand chords can be rolled from the bottom up to imitate a strummed guitar. Practice incorporating all the solo piano styles we've discussed into your own repertoire. Listen to the masters. And, as always, practice in all keys!

Part 4 - Latin Accompaniment

I'm using the term 'Latin rhythms' to cover everything from the bossa nova, to the bolero, to the rumba, to Afro-Cuban, to the cha-cha-cha, to Salsa and beyond. The complexities of each of these different rhythmic patterns need to be studied on their own. Try and find books on latin drum rhythms, and study the clave beat for each dance category (I recommend the "Afro-Latin Rhythm Dictionary" by Thomas A. Brown, "The Salsa Guidebook" by Rebeca Mauleon and "Inside the Brazilian Rhythm Section" by Nelson Faria and Cliff Korman). The clave is always the clue to the right feel. Let's look at a couple of rhythms that you might encounter in a solo accompanying context.

BOSSA NOVA - Bossa Nova is one of the most common latin rhythms we will come across in our accompanying.

When we're trying to be the whole rhythm section all on our own, we need to cover the bass line pattern and the traditional guitar comping pattern. Here are some sample rhythms you can use for playing your right-hand chords.

Example 8a

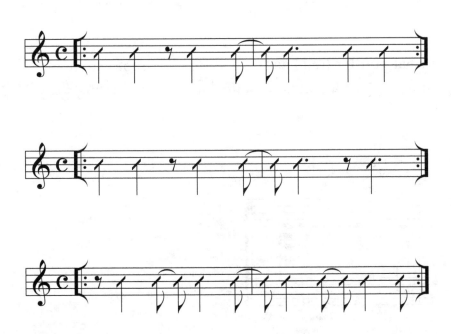

The bass lines in Bossa Nova are based on the rhythms of the "Surdo," which is a bass drum found in Brazilian Samba groups. This is the rhythm we'll use as our left-hand bass pattern. Most Brazilian bossa novas are actually written in 2/4. But since we're much more used to seeing them written in 4/4 in the States, that's how we'll notate them in these examples.

Example 8b - This is a typical bossa nova bass line.

Here's an example of how we can put it all together, still using "The Touch of Your Lips" as our source and proving once again the malleability of the American Songbook.

Example 8c

The Touch of Your Lips - Ray Noble

The bass line in example 8b is what you'll often hear played for a bossa nova but many of us prefer something simpler - just a simple 2 in the bar with half notes, thus...

Example 8d

"In terms of Brazilian music, I try to keep a simple bass line happening and that usually takes up everything my left hand is going to do. Most of the time I'll play block chords in the right hand and I tend to like sparse voicings; shell voicings, 3rds and 7ths, in a nice rhythm. Then I can bring in some melodic fills, still playing chords with my right hand. Of course what you really need is three hands. It doesn't have to be complicated. It can be real simple, even repetitious. In Brazilian music a lot of the appeal is the beautiful harmonies: That's what I concentrate on."
Larry Dunlap (pianist with Dame Cleo Laine, Mark Murphy, Bobbe Norris)

SAMBA - Samba's are definitely in 2 instead of 4 and can be thought of as faster Bossa Novas. The right-hand pattern is similar, but the bass is simpler. In order to continue using "The Touch of Your Lips", in this example we'll double the time and make the melody into a [35]*long form* in order to fit the faster tempo and yet not seem rushed. This is a great arranging trick if you're faced with a singer wanting a "lively feel" to a song. It enables you to double the tempo of the rhythm section and yet keep the melody in it's original form.

Example 8e

31

Many of the Latin dances can find their way into a singer's repertoire, from rumba to cha-cha-cha, to bolero. There are myriad styles of Latin music that can take a lifetime to learn, from Afro-Cuban to many forms of world music. It's unusual to face these complex rhythms in a solo situation, but studying them is an invaluable musical asset. I highly recommend listening to the wonderful Caribbean jazz pianist Monty Alexander. Look for him on youtube playing solo piano on a song called "Jamento." In just a few notes he conjures up the whole world of Latin music.

More Latin Listening (suggested by Larry Dunlap)

Cesar Camargo Mariano - For elegance and intelligent musical choices, mainly
　　　accompanying Elis Regina or Nana Cayman.
Ivan Lins and Antonio Carlos Jobim - For simplicity and essential perfection.
Hermeto Pascoal - For innovation, freedom and a deeply intuitive musical soul.

Part 5 - Up-Tempo Accompaniment

When you're playing solo piano accompaniment, you have to hope that, unless your name is Oscar Peterson, the vocalist is not going to call [36]*Cherokee* with a quarter note = 240. But we do, even solo, have to play faster tempos. If it's a Latin feel, the samba interpretation that we used in example 8d is a good way to go. It's fast and yet clear and succinct. There's a well-defined bass line, and the harmony in the right hand supports the melody. If the fast tune demands a swing feel, there are many tricks we can use to support the vocal without flailing around the keyboard trying to play a million notes. Remember, our job is to keep good time and lay down that carpet for the vocalist.

PEDAL POINTS - A pedal point can give the feeling of double time without being technically taxing. In classical music, a pedal point is a sustained tone, but in jazz we usually use the term to mean a single tone repeated in some rhythmic way beneath moving harmony. Here's how it might look accompanying a swinging 'Honeysuckle Rose.' I've put the pedal point on the off-beat to give us some rhythmic tension.

Example 9a

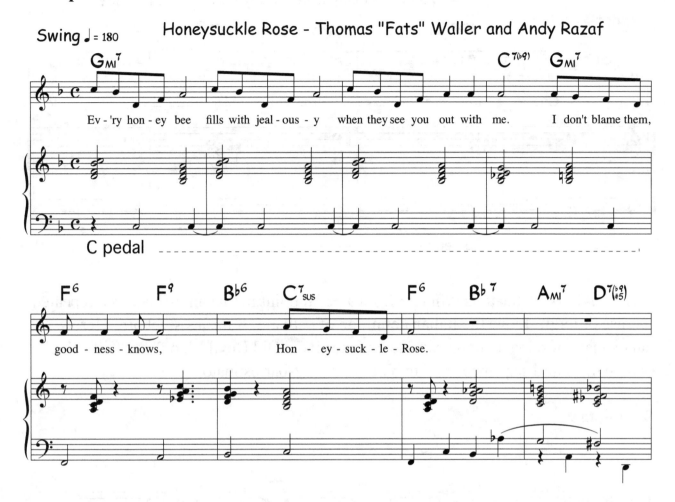

Notice that at the turn-around in bars 7 and 8, I've gone back to a walking bass line. But it's combined with what I call a *tenor line*, which means a melodic inner voice that usually occurs in the tenor tessitura. It starts on beat 4 in the 7th bar and is based on the seventh of the Bb7 and Ami7 and the third of the D7 chord. Play it with the thumb of your left hand and bring it out as if it were a melody line.

Pedal points are single tones that the harmony floats over. In the case of "Honeysuckle Rose," the harmony is a simple II-V-I. But the beauty of a pedal point is that you can get adventurous and use harmony that can be quite dissonant.

The original changes to our next pedal point example, "A Wonderful Day Like Today," are actually a very dull Ab for all of the first 4 bars. But with a pedal point and some interesting harmony, we can transform it into something exotic and swinging.

33

Example 9b

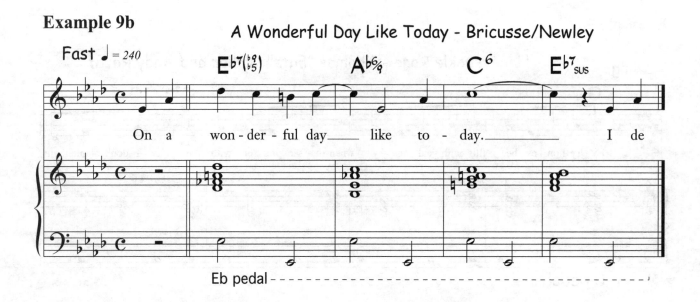

A Wonderful Day Like Today - Bricusse/Newley

Fast ♩ = 240

On a won-der-ful day____ like to-day._____ I de

Eb pedal -

OSTINATO - Ostinato is different from a pedal point in that an ostinato is a repeated phrase or motif. I love the Italian definition of ostinato. It means stubborn! Here's an ostinato of mine that you can use on tunes like "Old Devil Moon" or "Killer Joe" where the chord sequence is I 7 to bVII 7. It's a 2-bar ostinato.

Example 9c

When playing fast and the tune calls for a "swinging" accompaniment, you can use the walking bass line to good effect. Just make sure you spend some time studying great bass players, and try to construct interesting and musical bass lines. Anything Ray Brown played is perfect!

Part 6 - Show Style

Even though we're concentrating on accompanying for the jazz pianist, there are many techniques we can steal from the theater world. One of those is in playing what I can only describe as the "oom-pah" style, but it's very useful in up-tempo situations that might be beyond a comfortable walking bass line. The oom-pah style (it doesn't have to be corny) consists of a bass note with an off-beat chord in the right hand. Here's how it might be applied to Cole Porter's "Just One Of Those Things." This style gives us many opportunities for what I think of as 'tenor lines.' These are melodic lines, shaped by the harmony, and occurring in the the tenor tessitura. In this case it's the G and F# in bars 3 and 4.

Example 9d - Play them with your left-hand thumb and bring them out.

Part 7 - General Principles of Solo Accompaniment

The biggest hurdle to overcome with solo piano accompaniment is the panicked voice in your head saying, 'I'm going to have to play everything myself,' and then, unfortunately, proceeding to play everything. I find the hardest thing to achieve in our kind of "mainly improvised" music is the mental discipline to not overplay. Whether it stems from an egotistical point of view, the 'I have to show off my fabulous technique' syndrome, or from an attack of nerves due to a lack of self-confidence, overplaying is the most common fault of the solo accompanist. This can also apply to 'musical theater' situations where one is usually required to play exactly what's on the page. But it can still be prudent to edit your playing as you go in order to provide the cleanest accompaniment one can.

So how can you deal with this tendency to want to play too much? One way is to be secure and confident in what you plan to play, and that means careful preparation. That preparation, from a practical standpoint, won't always be possible for specific musical circumstances because so much of our work as accompanists is sight-reading, either at rehearsal or on the gig, with only the bare bones of what we're expected to play actually written on the page. Therefore you need to practice as many of those musical situations that you think you may encounter before getting to the gig.

Those musical situations will start with the basic voicing of all common chords and chord sequences. After all, that's what we're doing, laying down a harmonic carpet to support the vocalist. Practice all the basic harmonic patterns that occur in jazz and the American Songbook—for example, the ubiquitous I-vi-ii-V sequence—and practice them in all keys.

Here's an exercise (mainly referring to intros) that I give my accompanist students to help with achieving that goal. It's basically an ear training tool, but it's also useful as a tool to get you comfortable playing in every key. First, each exercise gives you specific ideas about what notes you might choose to play over a particular chord sequence, and then you get to apply your own taste, your own notes, and your own chord voicings, using only your ears! It's jazz after all. We're improvisors!

Let's start (example 10a) with a basic I-vi-ii-V intro. We'll imagine that we're using it as an intro to a rubato verse. Practice this passage, and get the sound of the sequence in your head. Then, hide the music and try and approximate the sound and feel of this passage up ½ a step, in Gb. Then try it in G, etc., etc. There's no need to remember the exact notes in each written example, or the exact melody. We're just trying to develop the ear and train our fingers to play these types of chord sequences in any key, so that when the vocalist says, "Give me a 4 bar intro in F... no, wait, I'm feeling really warmed up tonight, make it Gb," you're prepared!

Example 10a

Play freely - not too fast
Strive for eveness of tone

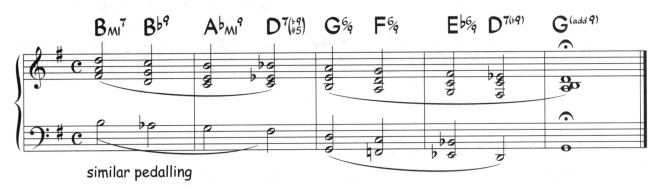

Here's another example, this time in G. Get the sound of this passage in your head and then try it in Ab.

Example 10b

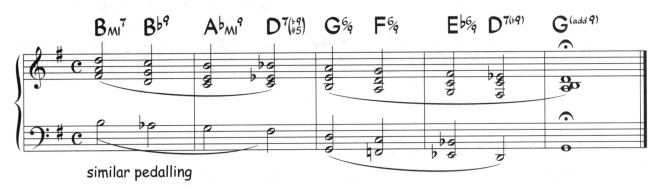

similar pedalling

Example 10c, introduces a more melodic approach to a series of ii-V's. After you've learned this one as written, try to approximate it in Db! It doesn't matter if the melody notes aren't the same. It is only important that it sounds harmonically similar to the original, only now in the new key of Db.

Example 10c

Now you can use the harmonic knowledge that your ears have absorbed to invent your own intros in any key. Try to invent melodic lines of your own similar to Example 10c. Often the reason we invent our own melody for an intro is because, as we've mentioned before, there are many singers who don't want the melody of the song they're about to sing telegraphed to the audience by anything that the pianist plays in the intro. This applies not only to you as the piano player, but you the arranger as well.

Let's try a similar exercise, but applied to swinging, medium tempo tunes. These are to be played in strict tempo. Again, strive for evenness of tone and lightness of touch. Make it swing! And then, as before, play them by ear in another key!

Example 11a

This final example (11b) utilizes the "pedal tone" we talked of earlier in this chapter. It's a very useful technique, especially when the intro involves the instruction, "vamp 'til ready."

Example 11b

A final thought on solo accompanying. Whenever anyone asks me who to listen to when talking about this art of accompanying singers, I always say, "listen to the singers who play for themselves!" You'll be amazed at how little they play. The list is lengthy and important—Fats Waller, Nat "King" Cole, Ray Charles, Mose Allison, Carmen McCrae, Shirley Horn, Sarah Vaughn, Bobby Short, Blossom Dearie, Jimmy Rowles, Diana Krall, Harry Connick and many more. And I want to encourage you, no matter how raspy or unattractive your voice may be, to practice by singing songs and accompanying yourself. I guarantee you won't be playing any intrusive arpeggios or busy hot licks while you're trying to support your own vocal efforts.

"Every singer is different, but the basis of playing for each one is the same. Pianists have a problem of how much to play. They shouldn't play too much. And there are questions of taste and how much to hold back. Holding back is especially important. But how much? Carmen taught me that all singers can put the chords in the right place for themselves; any singer can do it better for him/herself than any accompanist. The singer knows exactly what they're feeling. So she told me to listen to singers who play for themselves. I did that and got a wonderful foundation for accompanying. You realize how little they're doing - and what's actually needed and what's superfluous."

Norman Simmons

(pianist with Carmen McCrae, Anita O'Day, Joe Williams, Sarah Vaughn, Helen Humes; as quoted in "American Jazz Singers" by Leslie Gourse - Quill 1984)

So the mantra is, be prepared, expand your toolbox, so that you can cover all the musical situations that might confront you and handle them with aplomb. The toolbox consists of complete harmonic knowledge, the skill to play in all keys, a well-developed ear and a familiarity with the repertoire of the Great American Songbook. And most essentially, listen to the great master accompanists. From Teddy Wilson to Jimmy Rowles, to Ellis Larkins, to Tommy Flanagan, to Hank Jones, to Norman Simmons, to the best of todays accompanists—Bill Charlap, Mike Renzi, Lee Musicker, Christian Jacob, Eric Reed, Tedd Firth, Ted Rosenthal, Larry Dunlap, Richard Rodney Bennett, etc. You may not recognize all of those names (and I've left so many out) because the best accompanists are not always the most famous jazz stars of the day. Accompanying is a special skill and one in which piano players often toil in relative obscurity.

Listening - Instrumental Duos

It can be very informative for the vocal accompanist to listen to instrumental duets, always keeping in mind the different needs of vocalists compared to horn players.

Stan Getz & Jimmy Rowles - "Peacocks" (Jimmy also sings on this one)
Bill Evans & Jim Hall - "Undercurrents" (For those of you with adventurous singers)

GLOSSARY

1. World War 3 - Playing too many notes, much too loudly!

2. Voice Leading - In musical composition, voice-leading is the term used to refer to a decision-making consideration when arranging voices (or parts); that is, how each voice should move in advancing from each chord to the next. I also love this Wikipedia definition - "Voice leading may be described as parsimonious if it follows 'the law of the shortest way', moving as few voices as few steps as possible and therefore often retaining 'common tones.'"

3. Sing - " Thinking orchestrally will also help make your melodic lines sing. " In this context I don't mean literally that you "sing" the note but that, by using your touch and innate soulfulness, you make the melodic line beautiful and soaring, and therefore separate it from the accompaniment.

4. Escape Mechanism - When you press a piano key, two things happen: (1) a damper moves away from the strings for that note so they can vibrate freely, and (2) a hammer strikes the strings. Now, if the mechanical connection between key and hammer was a simple lever, then the hammer would strike the strings and remain in contact with them as long as you held down the key. That would prevent sustained vibration of the strings. Imagine the muffled "thunk" you would hear if, for example, you pressed your hand down on a guitar's strings and kept it there. To make a sustained sound, you need to touch the strings and then move away.

The piano's escapement mechanism is the clever solution to that problem. Just an instant before the hammer strikes the strings, it "escapes" its connection to the key so that it can strike the strings and then fall away from them, allowing them to continue to vibrate. It's almost as if the key "throws" the hammer, and the hammer bounces off the strings. Bartolomeo Cristofori is generally credited with inventing this mechanism and building the first pianos around 1710. The double escapement mechanism was invented by the Erard brothers in 1821, which allowed the same note to be repeated very quickly.

5. Touch - It's often said about piano players, "He/she has a lovely touch." What does that mean? Well, music isn't just about technique. It's also about feeling. Someone who has a nice touch is getting out of this inanimate object, the piano, the essence of the music being played. And touch is much more than a case of playing loud or soft. It's a case of wresting the emotion from the the keys. Forget about what your fingers are doing and play from the heart!

6. Time - Literally keeping good time, not slowing down or speeding up. An essential skill for the accompanist, especially when playing solo. Often in jazz, having good time can mean something more mysterious than just having a steady beat. It often means that feeling of propulsion that is the essence of good swing.

7. Sustain pedal - A sustain pedal or sustaining pedal (also called damper pedal) is the most commonly used pedal on a modern piano. It is typically the rightmost of two or three pedals. When pressed, the sustain pedal "sustains" all the damped strings on the piano by moving all the dampers away from the strings and allowing them to vibrate freely. All notes played will continue to sound until the pedal is released.

8. *Legato* - Term used to indicate performance without any perceptible interruption between the notes.

9. *Soft Pedal* - The soft pedal (or una corda pedal) is one of the standard pedals on a piano and is placed leftmost among the pedals. It allows you to play at a lower volume.

10. *Overtones* - An overtone is any frequency higher than the fundamental frequency of a sound. The fundamentals and the overtones together are called partials. Harmonics are partials whose frequencies are integer multiples of the fundamental. Phew… BTW the definition of integer is "a whole number; a number that is not a fraction". This subject is one worth looking up in a good musical dictionary, especially for the mathematically inclined!

11. *Walking* - When the bass player is playing a note on each beat of the bar in a swinging manner.

12. *Sides* - In the days of 78's and then later on, vinyl records, each side of the disc was known as Side A and Side B. Therefore 'sides' was jazz slang for a recorded track.

13. *Stride Piano* - Jazz piano style that was developed in the large cities of the East Coast, mainly New York, during 1920s and 1930s. The left hand characteristically plays a four-beat pulse with a single bass note, octave, seventh or tenth interval on the first and third beats, and a chord on the second and fourth beats. Occasionally this pattern is reversed by placing the chord on the downbeat and bass note(s) on the upbeat. Unlike earlier ragtime pianists, stride players' left hands often leapt greater distances on the keyboard, placing the chord at least an octave and a half to two octaves above the bass note.

14. *BeBop* - Bebop or bop is a style of jazz characterized by fast tempos, instrumental virtuosity and improvisation based on the combination of harmonic structure and melody. It was developed in the early and mid-1940s. It first surfaced in musicians' argot some time during the first two years of American involvement in the Second World War. BeBop was fomented in NY at Minton's Playhouse.

15. *Long Form* - The value of all the notes of a melody all doubled in length.

16. *Cherokee* - Bebop flag-waver made famous by Charlie Parker. The tune is in Bb and the 'a' sections are simple, but the bridge goes through 4 different keys - ii-V-I in B— ii-V-I in A— ii-V-I in G— ii-V-I in F. Yikes!

CHAPTER 3

The Art of "Out of Tempo" Accompaniment

The purists among you might wonder why I've used the English phrase, 'out of tempo' to describe this chapter. *Colla voce* - rubato – freely - out of tempo – *a suo arbitrio*, these are all terms that you'll find on charts to indicate that the passage is played without strict time-keeping. Actually, I've never seen "*a suo arbitrio*" on a chart, but I found it in my iPhone musical dictionary, and it means—'*Ad Libitum,* at will as to time, the choice of the degree of movement being left to the performer.' That definition is, in fact, perfect. It's exactly what we do when accompanying a singer who is phrasing freely.

Here are the definitions of the official musical terms.

Colla Voce - is an Italian term meaning, 'with the voice': implying that the accompanist must accommodate and take the time from the singer.

Rubato - is defined as 'stolen or robbed' and means, taking a portion of the duration from one note and giving it to another. Therefore rubato can also be applied to strict tempo passages and is often at the heart and soul of classical interpretations. But it's not really a good term for our style of 'out of tempo' playing - though you'll often see it used to describe such passages.

Of course "freely" and "out of tempo" speak for themselves.

Let's face it, it's out of tempo!

And this brings up an important point, if a passage is out of tempo then make sure it's performed out of tempo. Encourage the singer to phrase in a more conversational manner. Inexperienced singers will often not alter their phrasing at all when faced with an out of tempo passage, so the vocal line sounds like it's being sung in tempo but just slower! Remember, in our style of music the written note is just a guide, and we can manipulate it in anyway we choose.

Accompanying "Out of Tempo" Verses

There are many reasons for the arranger and singer to utilize 'out of tempo' passages, but the two main ones are;

  a: to enable the singer to tell the story of the lyric in a conversational manner.
  b: to provide dramatic contrast in relation to the 'in tempo' passages.

Whatever terminology is used to denote 'follow the singer in a free manner,' it is most often encountered in the singing of verses. Verses aren't done as often as they should be! As I said in the first chapter, I love verses. They often sound like miniature art songs, and much of the time it's in the verse that there's more opportunity for harmonic experimentation from the composer and/or arranger.

> *A little aside here; let's look at the definition of verse and chorus in popular songs. The definitions have changed from era to era. Most popular music, up until the early 1960's, was published with a verse and chorus set-up. This comes out of the Broadway tradition of using the verse as an extension of dramatic dialogue in order to set up the story and then segue into the more catchy (at least melodically) chorus. The verse sets up the premise of the story we're about to hear, sort of filling in the sub-text of what our main character is about to tell us in the chorus. It's a hip recitative, and the composer will often be much more adventurous melodically because there's less need of a 'popular hook.'*
>
> *In the 60's, at the start of the singer/songwriter era, the term 'verse' often came to mean what I think of as the chorus. Hence all this confusion. For example, someone says, "Bob Dylan wrote three verses to that song" when the song actually has, in my mind, three choruses. Anyway, all you really need to know is that when I'm talking about a verse, I mean it in the old fashioned sense, "that part of the song following the introduction and preceding the chorus."*

Well, even though I said that verses, from the composer's point of view, are a good place for harmonic experimentation, playing of all those delicious chords can also get us into trouble. When I first fell in love with harmony, I wanted to use every interesting chord change and substitution I could get my hands on. But this is not always the best path to take when accompanying. Our task is to assist the singer's storytelling. Putting a chord on every beat or every other beat can handcuff the singer and restrict their phrasing. We must remember that this style of music is a [37]*colloquial* art, and we want the singer to be as conversational as possible when singing out of tempo.

"I like to sing the words as if I was talking to someone."
Shirley Horn (jazz singer supreme)

Here's a simple example using the first four bars of the verse to 'The Lady's In Love With You' by Burton Lane and Frank Loesser. This is what the original sheet music looks like...

Example 1a

It all looks pretty simple and uncluttered, so when accompanying this verse, one would presume that all the chords should be played. But that's not necessarily the case. If the singer is smart, they will shape the phrase in a conversational manner, emphasizing just one word in every phrase, just as we speak. In the above lyric, let's say the singer's chosen to emphasize the word *'seen.'* Speak this phrase aloud, emphasizing *'seen.'* Do you find yourself hurrying over *'Have you ever'* to arrive at *'seen,'* holding *'seen'* a little and then hurrying along again through *'the dawn of love'*? If that's how the singer decides to phrase it, then we will need to make some editorial decisions on where to place the accompanying chords and which chords we'll choose to use.

If we insist on playing the Dmi7 on beat 3 of the first bar, the vocalist is forced to wait for us. This can result in a ponderous performance with the vocalist having to put equal emphasis on each beat—a habit that we try and beat out of all our vocal students! But we're creative jazz musicians, and the written music of example 1a is only a guide. Music does have to be notated in order to inform us of the composer's intent, but to bring the page to life, we sometimes need to take liberties with the composer's intentions. Back to our verse—here's how I would recommend editing this particular passage.

Example 1b

The Lady's In Love With You - Burton Lane & Frank Loesser

One of the reasons we can do this is because the Dmi7 that had occurred on beat 3 of the first bar isn't really going to be missed. F6 and Dmi7 have all the same notes, and the melody fits either of them, giving us the freedom to edit and the singer the freedom to phrase without the encumbrance of waiting for the piano player to catch up!

Let's also look at the music in bars 3 and 4. Is it necessary to play all of those chords and make the vocalist wait to start the next phrase? Yes and no. I'm certainly not trying to stifle those little opportunities when we get to shine, but one needs to take into account whether the singer wants to get to the next part of the story quickly or is happy to wait for you. Some singers will tell you exactly how they want to phrase a passage, but some will just follow you. This is where your taste and judgement are important. You can help the novice vocalist navigate the scary waters of *colla voce*. And, of course, this is why we rehearse!

> *"Even advanced piano players will often fill too much during 'out of tempo' passages, and stop the forward motion of the vocal line."*
> **Madeline Eastman** - jazz vocalist

The discussion of those 'filler' notes in bars 3 & 4 of Example 1b brings us to a very important aspect of *colla voce* accompaniment and accompaniment in general—the use of silence. Silence is an essential dramatic and emotional tool in all of music. Mind you, I have to admit that it's less effective when playing in a noisy saloon, but within the confines of this book we're all at Carnegie Hall.

We can solve the dilemma of whether to play all those chords in bars 3 and 4 of Example 1b by not playing them at all. Instead of filling every space with music, we can use our powerful and dramatic tool, silence, as a musical punctuation mark in between vocal phrases.

Here's what that might look like…

Example 1c

The effect of omitting all those chords in bar 3 is to make it seem like we've cut out the 4th bar altogether in order to create this musical punctuation. In fact in Example 1c, I have cut it out in order to make my point clearer. The quarter note rest on beat 4 of the 3rd bar is, in fact, filling in for the whole 4th bar in Example 1a. The dramatic effect of that moment of silence helps the listener concentrate on the intent of the lyric and at the same time gives the vocalist the freedom to continue on with the next phrase without having to wait for us to finish playing some pretty fill-in.

> *"Carmen taught me about suspense. The space belongs to the singer. Carmen communicates with her music through space, too. If a pianist elaborates in a singer's space, the singer has to wait, and maybe the train of phrasing is broken. That's where taste and sensitivity come in; knowing where it's appropriate to elaborate. The audience should be able to hear what the singer's going to say next and not be diverted by a great piano embellishment."*
> **Norman Simmons**

We've learned how to edit ourselves when the melody is [38]*diatonic* and the harmony reasonably simple. But what happens when there are chromatic notes introduced into the melody? How do we navigate these dangerous waters? Here's the verse to Sammy

Cahn's and Paul Weston's lovely ballad 'I Should Care.' I've put it in Wesla's key of G major.

Example 2a

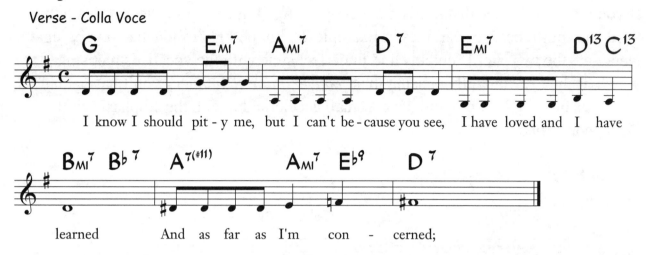

Verse - Colla Voce

I know I should pit - y me, but I can't be - cause you see, I have loved and I have

learned   And as far as I'm con - cerned;

The first three bars look pretty straightforward—diatonic with predictable harmony changes, so they shouldn't cause us too much trouble. But what about bar 5? The questions are: how should we voice the A7(#11), and should we play both the Ami and Eb7 on the beats 3 and 4 with the singer? After all, we just learned that we don't want to strangle the singer's ability to phrase naturally by forcing unnecessary chords on them. But bar 5 is quite a chromatic line, and we have to decide how much support the singer will need and how much we should stay out of the way. Some of this will depend on the ability of the singer. Can they negotiate these tricky half-steps with aplomb, or do they need some help? If they're confident, I'm all for letting them sing it on their own, and have the piano stay out of the way. . .like this.

Example 2b

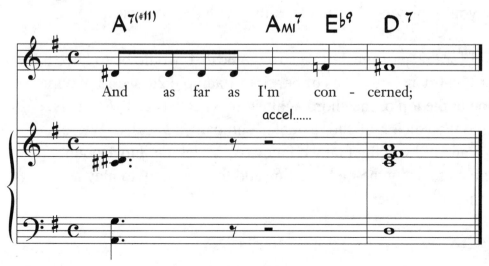

And   as   far   as   I'm   con - cerned;

accel......

Note that this is also one of those circumstances where we can break the 'no melody note on top of the chord' rule in order to give firm harmonic support to this 'out of key' melody line on the A7(#11) chord.

If you feel that the vocalist needs more support, by all means play the chords on the third and fourth beats of bar 5, as in Example 2c, but be light of touch and very legato. Negotiate the two chords quickly and in perfect sync with the vocalist's phrasing, which, if they're hopefully phasing in a [39]conversational manner, won't have equal emphasis on each beat but will have a small accelerando, with the emphasis on the lyric, 'concerned.'

Example 2c

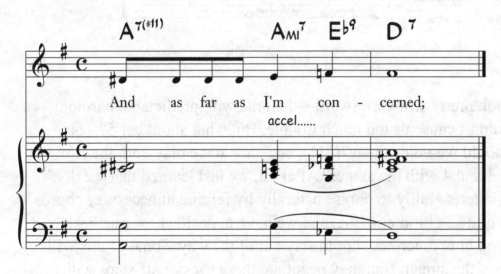

Notice that I mirrored the melody line on top of the chords in bar 5 in order to support the vocalist. But in bar 6, I didn't put the F# melody note of the D7 chord on top of my voicing. The third is so strong a note that doubling it just sounds like overkill and really does sound like you're playing the melody along with the vocalist.

In fact, the best voicing for this passage, with a strong vocalist, would be to have a [40]contrapuntal line for the 3rd and 4th beats of bar 5. In Example 2d, we're playing a B, Bb, A, melody line at the top of the chord against the vocalists E, F, F#. This is an important lesson in the voicing of chords that accompany a vocalist. We're not just plunking down any old voicing that we fancy. We're taking into account all the musical clues given to us by the melodic line and the harmony to play a complementary and musical statement.

Example 2d

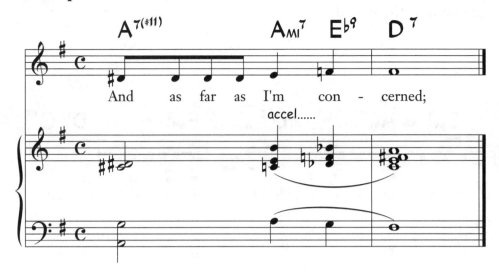

Before we leave "I Should Care," let's look at how the accompanist needs be acutely aware of the singer's phrasing. Let's say you're rehearsing and you hear something unusual in how the singer wants to phrase the verse. The commas (usually where the singer takes a breath) in the singer's phrasing don't quite fall where they are written in the lead sheet. (BTW one of the reasons the lyric line needs to be accurate on your lead sheet in these out of tempo passages is so that you can study the punctuation. Punctuation is a wonderful guide to predicting a singer's phrasing.) But in this case, the punctuation turns out to be different from what's written on the page, and we will need a new strategy.

This is how the lyric was written. . .

*"I know I should pity me, but I don't because you see, I have loved and I have learned. And as far as I'm concerne*d."

But in rehearsal we discover that our singer wants to do it this way!

*"I know I should pity me but I don't, because you see I have loved and I have learned. And as far as I'm concerne*d."

The second comma is now coming after *"don't"* instead of *"because you see."* This produces a wonderfully long and exciting phrase, *"because you see I have loved and I have learned. . ."* Speak these different punctuations, in a conversational way, and you'll get an idea of the singer's intent.

And so here's what we should do in order to accommodate this turn of events, keeping in mind the original placement of the chords.

Example 2e

Note the 1/8 note rest on the '*and*' of three in bar 2 - a wonderful moment of silence to prepare for the long phrase coming up. And because we're out of tempo, that 8th note rest can last as long as the vocalist likes, before continuing on with the next portion of the phrase. Note that I've simplified beats 3 and 4 in the third bar by changing the two written chords into a form of D7sus. Remember, we don't want to handcuff the singer in the middle of a long phrase by insisting on playing all the changes.

> *"With Carmen, it all comes together in her emotion, control and knowledge of the song. All singers say that the words are most important, that the story is, but they don't come out with the result. And the song is singing them. To sing the song they must pick up the high points within even a syllable to get across, not just the high point of the story. They must isolate a syllable, or a strong word, in some kind of way to get an audience reaction. They have to plan*

Our punctuation exercise in the last example demonstrates very subtle differences of phrasing from the original—differences that might not be apparent to the casual listener. But I want you to be aware of all the possible permutations of a singer's phrasing. It's this sort of critical thinking that can turn craft into art! Of course, you often don't have a rehearsal to work this sort of thing out intellectually. So you must rely on your ears and your instincts to create a smooth accompaniment while playing '[41]*in the moment.*'

Out of Tempo in the Middle of an Arrangement

Sometimes, for dramatic effect, in the middle of an arrangement we'll take a section out of tempo. Often it's the bridge of the song during the last chorus. Wesla feels that there has to be a good reason to sing a song through twice, so anything one can do to make it it different the second time is good. This tactic is most often applied to ballads. Why?

a. It's easier to get out of the tempo at a slow speed.
b. Ballad melodies are often more soaring and therefore more conducive to the dramatic reading that singing out of tempo can provide.

Taking a song out of tempo actually enables the singer to take the phrases at a faster pace, to 'trip along' so to speak, to be able to tell the story more convincingly in the middle of a slow ballad. We, as accompanists, have to make this transition as smooth as possible. First, we want to make it obvious that we're going out of tempo and not just fizzling out through lack of interest! Make sure that the rhythm section has a well defined stop so that the music doesn't just peter out, and then take a firm hand in whatever phrase you decide to play to guide the singer into the out of tempo passage. Here's what the piano part might look like going into the bridge of Jimmy McHugh and Johnny Mercer's great song "Don't Blame Me."

Example 3

Don't Blame Me - Jimmy McHugh & Johnny Mercer

I would play the eight notes in the left hand in bar 2 with a slight accelerando to indicate that something new is happening—then play the sixteenth-note run with a little *ritard* to bring out its lyrical properties. And don't forget to cut off the last chord to provide that split second of dramatic silence before the vocalist starts in on the bridge.

The first two bars of the bridge of "Don't Blame Me" bring up an aspect of chord voicing that I've often labored over, both as an accompanist and an arranger. The first chord of the bridge is C major, but the melody is very chromatic, so what should we play? We've already established that in most circumstances, we don't want to weigh down the vocalist's phrasing by attempting to play a chord on every beat they sing. Will it be OK if we just play a C chord and let the vocalist take care of the chromatic [42]*non-chord notes*? The answer is yes! You'll note that in voicing the chord, I haven't cluttered up the singer's territory, i.e. I've stayed clear of the tessitura of the melody. I've put the third of the chord an octave lower than I might in other circumstances.

But the enigma is that in the second bar of the bridge, the melody is also very chromatic, and the chord is B7. In this circumstance, it seems more pleasing to emphasize the altered note of the chord, the F natural rather than the F sharp. I'm not sure why this is—possibly because it's a dominant chord and not a tonic. Sometime

52

it's better not to question this sort of thing and just let your ear take over. If it sounds good, it probably is good!

To sum up, successful accompanying of 'out of tempo' passages demands all the subtle skills that define a great accompanist - great ears, musical sensitivity, sublimation of ego, the ability to breathe with the vocalist, along with the art of being a good editor.

Thoughts from the Pros on Rubato Accompaniment

"Rubato is, of course, all about following the singer. The singer should be focusing on the message of the lyrics and how to pace them most effectively. The vocalist doesn't need me to be suggesting pacing by what I play. If a singer wants to rush through a phrase, I'll be right there with them. To accommodate lyrics it sometimes requires simplifying the chord progression: the melodic phrase may not flow smoothly at a fast clip if I include all six written chords, so I'll take some out."

Randy Halberstadt

(pianist for Marlena Shaw, Kevin Mahogany, Sheila Jordan, Karrin Allison—quoted in "The Art of Accompanying Jazz Vocalists," thesis by Christopher Edward White)

"It's important to know the lyric. Carmen and I never discussed this topic, but she'd let me know that something was wrong by giving me the eye on stage."

Eric Gunnison

(pianist for Carmen McCrae—quoted in "The Art of Accompanying Jazz Vocalists," thesis by Christopher Edward White)

"I have dreams (nightmares) about accompanying someone I can't see...quite often singing songs I don't know. And sometimes they're mysteriously around the corner where I can't see them breathe. So you see, I have to see the vocalist breathe. I'm not watching their ribs like a hawk, but there's something about that physical connection with the vocalist."

Sir Richard Rodney Bennett

(pianist for Chris Connor, Dame Cleo Laine, Claire Martin)

"I find that if I can minimize the amount of connective tissue in the accompaniment, we're all pretty much better off. If you can keep the amount of filigree down, that can be very helpful. Now certainly if it's called for, that's fine. We're dealing with a specific kind of rubato that's an intimate kind of thing. Really let the melody do the heavy lifting. You're there to provide harmonic flooring."

Tedd Firth

(pianist for Marilyn Maye, Maureen McGovern, Brian Stokes Mitchell)

"Following and leading when playing rubato is conditional, and the accompanist should only lead when necessary."

Larry Dunlap

(pianist for Dame Cleo Laine, Mark Murphy, Bobbe Norris)

"Rubato is hard to predict. Many singers take more or less time to complete a phrase than I might expect. When I'm with a singer whose [time] feel is comfortable for me, it can be like a mutual mind-reading exercise where we're both responsive and sensitive to one another. Generally, the better the singer, the easier it is to follow in rubato episodes. A good singer will also allow the give and take that lets them lead and be lead within a few phrases."

John Colianni

(pianist for Mel Torme—quoted in "The Art of Accompanying Jazz Vocalists," thesis by Christopher Edward White)

"Rubato is really a question of matching your music flow with the singers flow. The singer has to deal with lyric deployment, which you don't, so you have to let them lead, but you have to keep an eye on the flow so as not to let it die."

Christian Jacob

(pianist for Tierney Sutton, Betty Buckley)

"You must let the drama of the song matter to you as an accompanist. I can't change the chord 7 times in a short passage, because it's going to completely obliterate the singers ability to render the proper meaning from the lyric."

Christopher Denny

(pianist for Karen Mason, Julie Wilson)

"Playing rubato for a singer is a delicate dance: It's an organic process. But it must be done with confidence." **John McDaniel**

(pianist for Patti LuPone, Rosie O'Donnell)

GLOSSARY

1. Colloquial - adjective: (of language) used in ordinary or familiar conversation; not formal or literary.

2. Diatonic - Designation for the major (also minor) scale as opposed to the chromatic scale. Also applied to melodies and harmonies confined to the notes of these scales, to the exclusion of the chromatic tones. For instance in C major C-D-E is diatonic, C-D-D#-E is chromatic.

3. Conversational Manner - Singing and phrasing rubato passages as if one were talking. (i.e., communicating in a colloquial fashion). When Wesla does master classes she often gets the student to speak the lyric, as if it were lines in a play, and then sing the phrase in exactly the same manner.

4. Contrapuntal - In the style of counterpoint (i.e., music consisting of two or more melodic lines sounding simultaneously). The term comes from the Latin *contrapuctus*, properly *punctus contra punctum*, meaning "note against note" or, by extension, "melody against melody."

5. In the Moment - Being aware of everything musical that's happening around you. Listening closely and not just focussing on your own performance.

6. Non-chord Notes - A non-chord tone or non-harmonic tone is a note in a piece of music which is not a part of the implied harmony that is described by the other notes sounding at the time.

CHAPTER 4

Duo and Trio Accompaniment

This chapter is really about the art of comping, how to voice those comped chords, and where and when to use melodic fills. That's mainly what accompanying consists of as soon as we add a rhythm section. Comping can be difficult to practice on your own because you have to imagine the bass player, the drummer and the vocal line all chugging along, even though they are not there. In fact, I highly recommend singing the vocal lines, because no matter how croaky you might sound, I assure you that you'll learn to play less and put the chords in the right place. You'll find out where you need support and where it's best to lay out. With today's notation software it's also possible for you to write out your own bass lines to a song (a good exercise), and play them back while you practice comping. Usually the first addition to a band, when we start to expand from solo piano accompaniment, will be a bass player.

The Duo - Let's Add a Bass Player

When we add a rhythm section, everything changes - especially that left hand! Remember all those things we studied in the last chapter to help your left hand be the foundation on which to build a solo style? Don't do that anymore! The bass player now has dominion over the roots of chords except—there's always an exception— when you want to double the bass note for a specific effect like a strong chordal downbeat or an accompanying unison riff. Doubling the bass note can be a very powerful arranging tool, but under normal circumstances, when we're comping over a walking bass, we avoid the root whenever possible. Why? Because in general we want to stay out of the other instrument's [43]*tessitura* to give a full and open sound to the ensemble. This is where all those hip Bill Evans voicings you've been practicing come to the fore.

As we've seen before in the solo accompaniment chapter, the piano can cover all aspects of music—harmony, rhythm and melody. But the more instruments one adds to the ensemble, in some ways, the less need there is for the piano player! In this case, we've added one instrument, the bass—(Don't forget that the vocalist is an instrument too.) This means that the melody is covered by the vocalist, and part of the harmony (the roots) and rhythm by the bass. That leaves us with the rest of the harmony and the syncopated rhythmic responsibility out of which to fashion our comping. Let's begin by taking a closer look at comping in general.

Comping: (an abbreviation of accompanying or complementing) is a term used in jazz to describe the chords, rhythms, and countermelodies that piano players use to support a jazz musician's melody lines or improvised solo. Comping is what the piano (or the guitar or vibes) is doing in a combo situation when they are not soloing (i.e., They are playing chords in a rhythmic manner behind the soloist). In our case, we're comping to support the vocal line. There are some similarities in approach and technique to comping for a jazz soloist; the main one being our old standby, listen, listen, listen. But there are many, many differences as well.

> *"I couldn't play behind Ella the same way I would behind a horn. Horn players would play the changes, but Ella, who is a very good musician, was more into the fixed melody. Ella required more subtlety. I was careful to provide accompaniment that was 'not out of context.' That's what you think about when accompanying. When Ella did ballads I couldn't go into a lot of alternate changes like you would with a horn. When you're sticking to a lyric and melody line, you have to stick pretty close to the pattern of the song."* **Tommy Flanagan** (quoted in "The Art of Accompanying Jazz Vocalists," Christopher Edward White)

For vocal accompaniment comping, there is another watchword over and above our 'listening' mantra, and that's - watch! Watching the singer breathe and move and gesture will also give you clues to their phrasing and indicate where you may want to place your chords. It's easier to anticipate a phrase when you're watching the singer take in a big breath than when you're lost in your own reverie with your eyes closed. I love this quote from the British classical accompanist Iain Burnside, "You build up a kind of musical radar. You become attuned to a singer's breathing. You get a sense of what their breath span is, and when they're likely to be heading for trouble. It's quite a private, sensual thing, listening to someone's breath that intently." Maybe that's why so many singers marry their accompanists!

Comping is a difficult art to teach in a book. Much of the learning must come on the bandstand through trial and error. Everyone's approach is quite different, and every singer's needs are quite different. There are as many styles of comping as there are piano players. It is, of course, important to listen to all the best players but also essential to find what style fits your own personal touch and technical prowess.

There was a time when a young player could go on the road with an established band and learn his craft. And speaking of learning on the bandstand, Tedd Firth had this to say about the fast-disappearing system of jazz apprenticeships. "Somebody came up with a phrase once that I thought was really good—that jazz is the most advanced form of folk music that there is, in that it is passed down by tradition as opposed to the classical tradition which is written down. It's an oral tradition and yet it functions, harmonically, melodically, and rhythmically, on a much higher level than your typical folk music. I think it's a cool way of putting it."

Before we get into examples of comping patterns, let's take a brief look at the different types of chord voicings that we'll utilize in our comping.

VOICING: Voicing is how we arrange the notes in a chord. When we talk about 'open voicing,' that means there's plenty of aural space between the notes being played. In 'closed voicing' the notes are, duh, close together. Of course then there are the hybrids. Like life, nothing in music is black and white. Hybrids are voicings that may be open for the bottom notes of a chord and closed at the top. Here's what these 3 types of voicings look like using a G7 chord. We are now presuming that the bass player we've added to the ensemble is playing a low G!

Example 1a

Use the open voicing when you want to provide a lush harmonic carpet for the singer, and use the closed voicing when a more rhythmic and percussive accompanying style is needed. And of course, as always, you have to take into account the vocalist's melody note! As we talked about in chapter 1, there are times when you want to stay away from the vocalist's note and times when you want to reinforce it.

Here's what our old friend the C6/9 chord looked like in the solo piano chapter followed by how to voice it when we have a bass player. It's so simple. We just don't play the root!

Example 1b

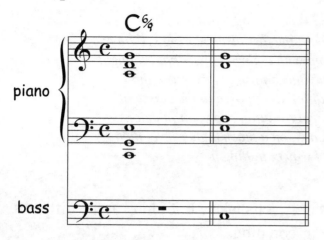

The voicing in example 1b, is built on 4th's, and I suppose it's quite modern sounding —although it's interesting for me to remember that what was revolutionary in 1960 is now accepted by our contemporary ears as quite normal. Bill Evans was the master of this sort of voicing. I still remember the revelatory feeling I had when I discovered I could play G13 with just the 7th, 3rd and 13th. Here's a typical way to use that style of voicing. The bass is playing the root, the left hand is playing that hip voicing, and the right is playing a melodic fill. As with all these examples, experiment in all keys and invent your own [44]*licks*.

Example 1c

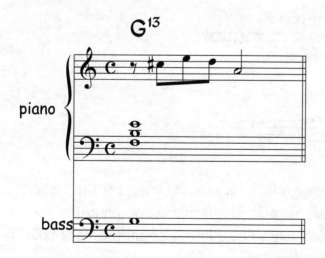

"With vocalists, I play more 'spread' voicings using widely-spaced intervals like stacked 5th's e.g. C G A D. It allows more space and breathing room for the vocalist. I use fewer clusters for the same reason and comp less aggressively overall." **Eric Gunnison** (quoted in "The Art of Accompanying Jazz Vocalists," Christopher Edward White - Thesis)

Your choice of chordal voicing is important because the colors of the chords you play will evoke particular moods. And those moods may change from moment to moment in a song. Open and expansive voicings will provide a lush and romantic mood. Clusters can provide tension and drama. Of course, the effects of all voicings are dependent upon your dynamics and touch. A lush voicing played staccato and loud will have a very different effect from one that is played sustained and softly.

Example 1d - Here are some examples of chord voicings that evoke quite different moods.

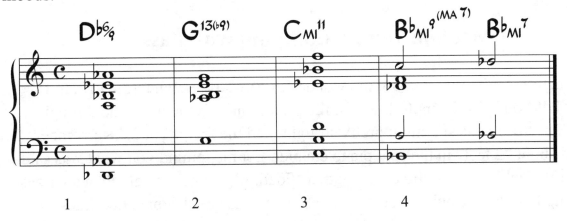

1. The Db6/9 is warm and rich. By the way, keys seem to have very different mood and colors, and that phenomenon should be taken into account when choosing keys for a song. There's a reason that Billy Strayhorn wrote "Lush Life" in Db. It suits the dark mood of the song. Marian McPartland liked to designate a color to all of the keys. She called D major 'daffodil yellow,' and it's true, D major is a sunny, airy key.

2. I think of the G13(b9) as an F diminished chord with the added G and E—very mysterious.

3. This voicing of a Cm11 chord is usually known as (according to Mark Levine's great book, "The Jazz Piano Book") the Kenny Barron voicing. It consists of stacked 5ths in each hand separated by by a half-step. It has a wonderfully poignant sound.

4. This is basically a Bbm, but it shows how moving just a couple of notes within a chord can alter the mood. The resolving of the 9th and the major 7th to the minor 3rd and 7th makes us feel that we're moving from a great uncertainty to inner peace. Well, music is meant to be poetic.

The comprehensive study of jazz harmony is too large a subject for this book, so get out your jazz harmony books and experiment with different voicings of chords—practicing them in all the keys—all the while hearing the bass player, in your head, laying down a solid foundation.

(I recommend the above mentioned "The Jazz Piano Book" by Mark Levine, and "A Creative Approach to Jazz Piano Harmony" By Bill Dobbins)

Medium Tempo Comping with Bass

For this section, we're going to use the wonderful Ray Noble standard, "I Hadn't Anyone 'Till You." In Example 13a, I'm imagining that it's the first time through the tune. The vocalist is singing it pretty straight, and the feel is "in 2." Remember we talked about "2 feel" in the solo piano chapter. Let me remind you what was said. "With a 'two feel,' we're trying to create that 'floating' feeling we get when a bass is not walking but playing only on beats 1 and 3 with occasional connecting lines."

"For me, unless four is played masterfully, two swings more! Now there's something that I call playing in '3'. I was discussing this with the great bassist Jay Leonhart—In other words, you're playing in two, but the bass might play, one, rest, three, rest, one, rest, three four. So you're not playing all the quarters. It's a modified two, but it gives you the feel of two."
Lee Musiker

In Example 2a, on the following page, in order to establish a rich harmonic carpet, and therefore provide the vocalist with the proper support, I'm playing [45]*on the beat* in measures 1 and 2 and not comping rhythmically. In measure 3, I needed more interest and rhythmic propulsion because nothing is happening in the vocal line. So this comping is more rhythmic and more percussive in the voicing.

Example 2a

Let's also look at measure 3 from a jazz phrasing standpoint. Sometimes phrasing marks will be shown on a jazz charts, but more often than not, they won't be shown. But because of tradition and experience, the professional will probably know how to phrase any particular rhythmic pattern. Measure 3 sets up to be phrased like this….

Example 2b - (note the short and long articulations)

When voicing chords for comping, it's amazing how little of the left hand one often uses. In Example 2a, most of the time I'm only playing one note with my left hand — it's easy! Measure 3 is in a style called "locked hands" first used by Mel Powell but made famous by George Shearing in his quintet. Basically the left hand doubles the melody line with closed voicing harmony filling in between.

There's a variation on this block chord voicing called 'drop two' — the simple principle being that you take a 4 note chord in closed voicing and drop the second note from the top down an octave. If we did that, measure 3 in example 2a would look like this (following page)…

Example 2c

In Example 2d, let's imagine that it's the last chorus of the song, and things are swinging. The bass player is walking 4 to the bar, and the vocalist is improvising.

Example 2d

The first thing you might notice in this version is that the vocalist is "messing" with the melody and [46]*singing across the barline.* Hopefully, on the bandstand, you're listening intently and are hearing these alterations and reacting instantly! This time our comping in measures 1 and 2 is more rhythmic but still minimalist in the left hand. And because I'm intently listening to the vocalist 'sing across the barline' in measure 3, I've delayed filling that space until beats 3 and 4. This time the fill is more of a single note line with the chords being played in the left hand. And in measure 4, notice that I'm mirroring the vocalist's melodic idea from the first two beats of measure 3. Always steal from the best!

Singing across the barline - This means that the vocalist is delaying the written phrase and extending it into a measure that was previously just a held note (see measures

3 and 4 in Example 2d and compare them to Example 2a). This is also called 'back phrasing.' Billie Holiday was an early master of this art. Singing behind the beat not only gives the story teller (our trusty vocalist) a new tool to interpret the lyric but also provides rhythmic tension, an important ingredient in swinging!

One of the important things to remember about comping is to try and constantly vary your harmonic and rhythmic approach to a repeating chord sequence. Find new ways around a recurring series of chords. Don't play the same pattern each time it occurs. You can practice this by taking a simple ii-V-1 sequence like say, Gm7 / C7 / | F / / / and try and find all the combination of voicings that fit well under your fingers. Remembering to take into account that in a real life situation we're also listening to the vocalist's melody line and the bass player's line! Here's just four examples of the endless variations of rhythms and voicings that you can invent over this ubiquitous ii -V-I chord sequence. Don't forget to practice this exercise in all keys!

Example 3a

Example 3b

Example 3c

Example 3d

Example 3a I'm using open voicing—our old friend 'drop two.' It provides a nice 10th between the top note of the chord and the single note being played in the left hand. Notice that although we talked about this being a Gm7 / C7 / | F / / / | sequence, I've added a flattened 9th to the C7 chord. The efficacy of this depends on what note is being sung by the vocalist. If the melody note of the song was a D natural, the flattened 9th would be inappropriate. These are decisions we make on the fly, using our ears, or by perusing the chart, but they are decisions that piano players like to make for themselves. As Bill Charlap said in an earlier chapter, he just needs basic chordal information, and he will decide what the coloring of the chord might be, according to the melodic situation and any extra information his ears are gathering in.

Example 3b I'm using closed voicing, i.e. the bottom note is doubling the top note, and the harmony is filled in between.

Example 3c This is more percussive comping, and we're utilizing octaves in the right hand. BTW, the technique I use to play the grace note in measure 1 is to let the thumb just slide off the G# onto the A natural. Not taught in [47]*Hanon*!

Example 3d This is a fuller and warmer style of comping, suitable for ballad playing. Again, those altered notes in the C7 chord will depend on the context!

I've mainly been talking about chordal comping so far, but comping is also a form of [48]*obbligato*, and so we can also use single-note melodic lines as a form of comping. In the jazz world, obbligato usually refers to an instrumental line that is an accompaniment and a counter-melody to the vocal line. It also refers to instrumental lines played between the vocal phrases. In the classical world, it's a whole other thing. See the endnotes (6) of this chapter for a full explanation. I had an eccentric jazz teacher named Red Price. Red was a great English tenor sax player. He would always say, "Hey, Mike, play some *obble gobble* behind the singer."

On the following page is an example of some single-note comping on Cole Porter's wonderful [49]*list song* 'At Long Last Love.'

Example 4

At Long Last Love - Cole Porter

This passage was transcribed from Wesla Whitfield's Cabaret Records CD "Beautiful Love" and wasn't, therefore, formally written out. It was improvised comping over the chord changes. Notice that I've come up with a melodic motif in measure 3 and then decided to repeat it in measure 5. But in measure 5, the chord is slightly different. It's a Gm6 instead of Gm7, and the vocal melody note is E natural. So, to avoid conflict with the melody, I've altered the 3rd note of the motif to a G instead of an F. This is just the sort of detail that points out the need to keep your ears wide open at all times.

Ballad Comping with Bass

The previous examples of comping are mainly intended for tunes taken at a medium tempo. Playing ballads with a bass player is a little different. We need to be very aware of our 'time', because it's so easy to speed up. And yet, we need to cover for the lack of aural atmosphere that a drummer often provides. I was surprised in going back to listen to a couple of piano/bass CD's I did with the [50]*missus*, Wesla Whitfield, how often I played '4 in the bar' with my left hand. If I'd sat down to intellectually think out a comping strategy for playing ballads, I probably would not have imagined that I would play that much on the beat—almost like a rhythm guitar. But there I was, using quite minimalist chords and saving the right hand for subtle melodic fills. Here's how that looks on the page.

Example 5a

The left hand needs to be legato and yet detached! Notice that I didn't fill in the first two measures melodically and that's because I wasn't sure when Wesla was going to come in! She was singing way behind the beat, and I didn't want to step on her entry when it finally did come. Here's how the tune is written and harmonized originally, so you can understand why I was waiting for her entrance. The melody starts on beat 1 of bar 1, and Wesla didn't start singing until the 'and of 1' in bar 2. There's one thing you don't want to do, and that's step on the vocalist's opening lines!

This minimalist approach to the start of the tune actually creates a wonderfully mysterious atmosphere, and has the audience wondering what's about to happen next. Remember, even though we, as accompanists, are playing music instrumentally, we're also in the story-telling business, and we can learn much from all the little dramatic tricks that playwrights, actors and directors use to create tension and release.

When the ballad is more bluesy, which often happens in the jazz oeuvre, our approach can be more rhythmic, even though the tempo is slow. This is also an effective approach when we're implying a [51]*double-time feel*. But be careful. Another of my pet peeves that I hear much too often, is the constant doubling of tempos in jazz ballads—most egregiously when the bass takes it up and starts walking in the double tempo! What's the point? But I digress yet again.... because, of course, the *implying* of double-time feel can be very exciting. Here's an example of that on the minor key ballad "You Don't Know What Love Is."

Example 6

A couple of things to note in Example 6: the octave Bb grace note on the 3rd beat of measure 1 is a typical "bluesy" device used in an attempt to, as they say, play in the cracks. As piano players, we can't bend notes or slide between tones like a horn player can. We must make up our own, often unorthodox, techniques of wringing the soul out of the unbending keyboard. In measure 2, we continue to use octaves in the right hand, and the articulations shown on beats 3 and 4 are meant to 'swing the beat.' They are accented *and* long ([52]*tenuto*), and yet there should be air in between each of them. This doesn't necessarily mean that they have to be played loudly. The technique of using octaves in this way is in the Red Garland style, a piano player everyone should listen to and inwardly digest. You know, sometimes the most swinging and hippest thing you can do is to play on the beat. Listen to how Louis Armstrong plays quarter notes!

Let's now look at an example of ballad comping that evokes a more spacious and languorous feeling. This example also gives us a heads-up on some of the arranging methods we'll look at in chapter 5.

Irving Berlin's "I Got Lost In His Arms" is written as a medium slow ballad in 4/4. It has a lot of repeated notes, and it's easy for it to sound plodding and ponderous, except in the most expert hands. I decided that it flowed better in 3 / 4.

Here's the original;

Example 7a

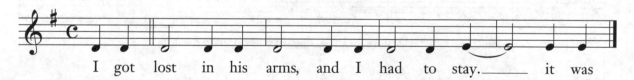

And here's what the phrasing looks like when we change it to a waltz.

Example 7b

. . . and here's what the accompaniment might look like.

Example 7c

First of all, note that I've broken one of my rules for accompanying when a bass is present. I'm doubling the bass note on a lot of the chords. Well, rules are made to be broken. Larry Dunlap told me that he had a teacher who used to say, "All's fair in love and theory." This is one of those circumstances where the reinforcement of the bass note is a good thing and not at all overpowering. It anchors the sound. The treble clef octave D in measures 1, 2 and 3—that occurs on beat 2—helps state the rhythm of the accompaniment and yet still maintains the airy/floating feel.

General Comping Strategies

When I started out accompanying I found it easier to find interesting ways to comp in passages where lots of chord changes were occurring. I had much more trouble when there was just one chord for 4 bars. What do we do? How do we vary our voicings? The same triad for 4 bars isn't going to cut it! On the next page are some ideas for what to play when you have 4 bars of F.

Example 8

In measure 1 - I've used our now very old friend, 'drop two' voicing. Again, this means that the second note down from the top of a closed-voice chord is dropped to the bottom of the chord. In this case, it also produces a nice warm sounding tenth between the top and bottom notes.

In measure 2 - I've gone back to closed voicing with the top note of the chord doubled in the bass. This can be used for more percussive comping.

In measure 3 - We're even more percussive, using octaves in the right hand, preceded by grace notes, making it more emphatic rhythmically, i.e. [53]*funky*.

In measure 4 - I've used closed-position voicing in the right hand and then doubled the same voicing an octave lower to make a more powerful and full sound. This tactic is often used in big band arranging where the trombones will double the trumpet voicing an octave lower, a very strong sound.

There are obviously thousands upon thousands of different combinations of rhythms and voicings that we can utilize. Practice different comping patterns in all keys, and find what best suits your style. And most importantly, try to not repeat yourself. Charles Mingus, the wonderful jazz bassist and composer, was famous for hating piano players who played the same rhythm, and the same voicing, in the same harmonic spot, in the same place, every time through the tune!

Of course, the caveat here, as always, is that what we play in any particular circumstance is going to be dictated by the melody. If the melody note is a repeated F, we're not going to hammer away on the major 7 as the top note of our voicing. That wouldn't help the vocalist one bit. Having said that, example 8 at least gives you some ideas for patterns and voicings that you can adapt to your particular challenge. Again, practice similar phrasing in all keys!

When comping with added instruments like the bass, it's best to stay within the middle range of the piano. Playing too low intrudes on the bassist's territory and can also sound muddy. Playing too high can be jarring and can stand out too much from the vocalist's line. The ideal range is from around G an octave and a fourth below middle C to G an octave and a fifth above middle C. I also try to think about the tessitura of the vocal line and stay away from that as well. I know... that doesn't seem to leave us much room. But remember, these are just guidelines that give us an idea of where and how we should be playing. But all these rules are probably meant to be broken.

We briefly leave the vocalist behind—it's time for a bass solo.

When you find yourself in a duo situation and you're playing for a jazz singer, (whatever that is, but that's a whole other book), there will be bass solos. Let's take a look at the best way of comping for bass solos. I have found that different bass players like different comping styles. Often the best thing to do is to ask the bass player what his/her preference may be. Some bass players will like you to [54]*lay out* completely and not comp at all, some will like your usual comping style, and some will like a combination of both!

> *It wasn't until I was writing this passage that I actually questioned my regular bassist, John Wiitala, as to his preferences in piano comping. John, being the diplomatic gentleman that he is, gave me a wonderful answer. He said that he hadn't thought about it before, so I must be doing it right!*

I have found that the best approach is to comp minimally, but when you do play, make sure you delineate the harmonic outline or form of the tune (i.e., show us, the audience and the band, the way). Indicate when there's a change of harmonic territory, and if the tune is in 8 or 16 bar segments, note those signposts as well. This approach is also helpful to the audience who, not being as harmonically sophisticated as we professional musicians, appreciate the aural road map that the piano comping provides. I know this sounds like I'm dissing bass players for playing meandering solos, but I certainly don't mean to at all. Many bass players have told me that they appreciate this approach, as long as it's subtle and not overbearing in any way. It's also important to take into account the range in which the bass player is soloing. If the solo is happening around the bottom end of the bassist's range, don't comp in the bottom half of the piano. It will cover up the bass player's sound.

Here's an example of comping for a bass solo on that old flag waver "How High The Moon." In case you're not familiar with the song, I've put the melody on the top just for reference.

Example 9

For some bass players, this might be a little too busy and possibly too obvious. But it does show you all the comping possibilities and I've hit all the harmonic signposts. If I did play Example 9 as written, after I'd hit the Eb chord in bar 9, I might lay out for the next 8 bars and wait until the second half of the tune to start comping again. ("How High The Moon" is written in two 16-bar sections). This initial comping has the effect of launching the bass solo, and then laying out produces another musical color—the piano player is finally shutting up!

So you can see from all these examples that there are many, many rhythmic permutations, voicings and styles that can be used in comping when we've added a bass player. But the best classroom is still the bandstand. By trial and error, find out what seems to best suit your own style and touch. Listen to everyone, and steal from the best. It's a very challenging and very satisfying art.

The Trio - Add Drums

The addition of a sensitive drummer (no drummer jokes here) will help us even more. By some sort of magic, the jazz trio—piano, bass and drums—is the perfect engine for a jazz performance. Adding drums to the piano/bass duo gives us a rhythmic lift and an aural completeness. When there was just bass and piano, we had to take a reasonably strong rhythmic role in our comping. But now, with the addition of drums, some of that role falls to the percussionist, and we're left with the freedom to paint our harmonic canvas in support of the vocalist in a more subtle way. Of course, most of the comping techniques described in the previous section will also apply to comping with a drummer in the mix. We're just not quite as responsible for providing such a specific and comprehensive rhythmic feel at all times. That's now the drummer's job.

From an arranger's standpoint, the addition of drums gives us more musical colors to choose from, and as a piano player, more freedom to play less.

> *The reason I'm tough on sound engineers, who want to put microphones all over a kit, is because, when accompanying vocalists, I feel I'm mainly a texture. How much I play depends on the style of the vocalist, of course, but I'm there for color and, of course, swing. It's like adding spice, putting things in the soup to make it bigger. Sometimes the music is so pretty the drummer doesn't need to be busy."* **Vince Lateano**
> (Mike G's regular drummer and *bon vivant*, married to the fabulous jazz singer, Madeline Eastman)

Let's think about comping with the trio when the drummer is playing brushes and the bass is playing in two. A good brush player will produce a swirl of subtle sound while still providing a steady beat. This allows the pianist the space to play whatever seems appropriate for the mood of the song. It can be floating, sustained chords or it can be choppy, rhythmic accents. As Lee Musiker said earlier, sometimes playing 'in 2' can swing more than a 'walking 4.' If you look back at Example 2a in this chapter, you can see the sort of comping that I'm referring to.

When the bass and drums are in a 'swinging 4', our approach to comping is more sparse and more rhythmic (see Example 2d). We are still, of course, supporting the vocal, but also pushing the band along, generating swing!

Fast tempos are easier and certainly more stable when we've added a drummer. A swinging drummer allows us to relax, pick our comping spots and not feel that we have to fill up every available space.

Latin rhythms are where the drums in a trio come into their own. They provide excitement and the authentic rhythm for the particular latin style being played, whether rumba, Afro-Cuban, cha-cha-cha, bossa or samba. Again, study all the Latin rhythms. This will aid not only in your playing, but also help when wearing your arranger's hat. *Recommended reading - Afro-Latin Rhythm Dictionary by Thomas A. Brown*

A brief look at ballad accompanying with drums: Shirley Horn could play a ballad so slowly that it seemed like she'd never get to the next beat. I often wondered how this was done, and I discovered the solution when I saw her live. I realized that the bass player was intently looking at her left hand in order to divine when she was going to play the next beat, and the drummer wasn't playing time at all! He was creating that wonderful swirl of sound with the brushes but not any particular beat. Of course this was all an illusion. Shirley, and her trio, had perfect time, however slow the tune.

Listening
Shirley Horn - "Lazy Afternoon" - Steeplechase
Shirley Horn - "Close Enough For Love" - Verve

One of the many hats an accompanist must wear, especially if he/she is also musical director, is to be the interpreter of the arrangement/chart being played—whether it is your own or someone else's. One of those duties is to instruct the drummer when to play brushes or sticks, or when to change from one to the other. Many arrangements will have these sort of instructions written in on the charts, but many will not. It is also, of course, up to the vocalist to have strong opinions on this matter. Drummers will find in accompanying singers that brushes are often the most used tools in his kit. That's because the brush sound is subtle and less intrusive than sticks. We want the drummer to give us all that wonderful verve and swing without covering up the vocalist.

The approach to comping for a vocalist is often quite different than comping for a jazz soloist. We need to play chords on "one" far more often than we would in a purely instrumental setting, where rhythmic variety and harmonic adventurousness is the rule. We do this in order to support the vocal line. Remember, the vocalist has to pull notes out of thin air and needs all the harmonic help available.

> *"If I play with an instrumentalist and I get the signal to solo, I show off. I mean I go in with the tune, but then I take off. When it's a singer who turns to me and gestures to solo, it's totally different in my head. It's like totally about the song. It's not about the solo at all. The solo's got to be a bridge to the next vocal entrance."* **Christian Jacob**

The Trio - Add Bass and Guitar

This has been a popular trio combination ever since the first Nat "King" Cole trio appeared on the scene - though when a guitar is added to a rhythm section we must beware. There are many pitfalls for the unsuspecting pianist to fall into because now we're faced with two chordal instruments. The question is, who's going to comp? The guitar in early ensembles, from the Count Basie Band to the Nat Cole trio, was usually used as a "4 in the bar" rhythm instrument. i.e., it kept time, while also taking care of harmonic duties. But it was not comping in the sense that we've been studying in this chapter (i.e. the choppy and rhythmic placement of chords to accompany a melodic line). This style of rhythm guitar provides a wonderful harmonic and rhythmic carpet and frees up the pianist who can play much more sparsely and melodically. This was the whole essence of the Count Basie rhythm section style, and Basie himself became the quintessential minimalist. But where disaster can occur is when both guitar and piano want to comp.

So if the guitarist is comping in the modern sense, keep your playing to a minimum. Use melodic fills, quick flourishes of sound, silence, and always listen intently. Be ready to swap roles with the guitarist at any time.

Listening
"Hit That Jive Jack" - Nat 'King' Cole - Verve
"All For You" - Diana Krall (A dedication to the Nat King Cole Trio) - Verve

GLOSSARY

1. Tessitura - "Describes the most musically acceptable and comfortable range for a given singer or instrumentalist. The range in which a given type of voice presents its best-sounding texture or timbre. In musical notation, *tessitura* is used to refer to the compass in which a piece of music lies— whether high or low, etc.—for a particular vocal (or less often instrumental) part. The *tessitura* of a piece is not decided by the extremes of its range, but rather by which part of the range is most used." Wikipedia (Hey, sometimes it's right!)

2. Licks - jazzy snippets of melody. Often personalized, as in, "I just copped all of those great Charlie Parker licks."

3. On the beat - Not syncopated.

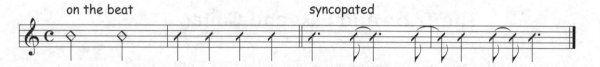

4. Singing Across the Barline - Displacing the melody, usually behind the beat.

5. Hanon - Charles-Louis Hanon (2 July 1819 – 19 March 1900) was a French piano pedagogue and composer, and author of a system of piano exercises. He is best known for his work "The Virtuoso Pianist in 60 Exercises," which has become the most widely used set of exercises in modern piano teaching.

6. Obbligato - A persistent but subordinate motif; A theme that is repeated or elaborated in a piece of music; A part of the score that must be performed without change or omission.

7. List Song - A song with a laundry list of subjects on a common topic. Cole Porter's "At Long Last Love" starts with a series of similar questions. "Is it an earthquake or merely a shock? Is it the good turtle soup or merely the mock? Is it a cocktail, this feeling of joy? Or is what I feel the real McCoy?" Other examples are, "Let's Do It", "These Foolish Things", "You're the Top."

8. Missus - Affectionate English term for one's female spouse.

9. Double-Time Feel - This is where the rhythm section implies, though doesn't state emphatically, that the tempo of the ballad has doubled. It can be achieved by the drummer being more aggressive, or the pianist comping as if the time was doubled, or the bass playing almost walking 4 in the double tempo.

10. Tenuto - Fully sustained, occasionally a bit longer than the note value requires.

11. Funky - Relating to music that has an earthy quality, reminiscent of the blues.

12. Lay-Out - Jazz slang for don't play!

CHAPTER 5

The Accompanist as Arranger (and Copyist!)

As accompanists, I would guess that 100% of us end up arranging songs for the singers we work with, and also writing out charts for the musicians. It's a skill that goes along with our many roles, such as musical director, confidant, artistic advisor, etc. First of all—the basics! What is an arrangement, and what is a chart? They are actually different, though the terms are often used interchangeably. The arrangement is the arranger's and singer's conception of how they are going to perform a particular song. The chart is the actual, physical road map for musicians to follow.

An arrangement can be as simple as a one-chorus reading of a standard, with no particular alteration to the original sheet music (except maybe the choosing of a suitable key and slight revision of the chord changes), to a complete reinvention of the song, (e.g., changing the meter, changing the form, putting the bridge where the verse is supposed to go, inventing an unusual rhythmic carpet, etc). Always keep in mind that the arrangement must serve the singer's ability to interpret the song and not just show off the arranger's cleverness.

There are a whole host of musical ideas that can be applied to this body of work known as the American Popular Songbook. As an aside, I think that this malleability (i.e., the ability to change and reshape a song without taking away any of the song's truth or meaning) is what defines the American Songbook. I'm often asked why we, Wesla Whitfield and I, don't perform more Stephen Sondheim. It's because his writing style, most of the time, demands that you perform the song exactly the way he wrote it, from the vocal line phrasing to the piano accompaniment. Therefore, it's hard to make those songs one's own. This is not to criticize Sondheim in any way, I adore a lot of his music, but to note that he's bit of a different animal from the one we are trying to tame in these pages.

Arrangements

An arrangement is the musical organization of a song's performance, a way to personalize the song, give it a new and fresh coat of paint! As I said, it can encompass everything from simply changing the meter, changing the rhythmic feel, changing the order of verse/bridge/chorus, changing keys, adding instrumental colors or altering the harmony. The purpose of the arrangement is to provide a wonderful and comfortable carpet upon which a singer can weave their spell. Common sense prevails here. Use your musical common sense. We don't want a busy rock 'n roll bass line underneath a tender Irving Berlin ballad.

All of this should be done with respect and admiration for the song. Like a doctor, "do no harm" should be our watchword. An arrangement shouldn't overwhelm the singer or the song. Just because you got your first opportunity to write for an orchestra, don't be tempted to use everything you've ever learned and end up writing Wagnerian bombast behind a sweet and tender passage. Always serve the song and the singer.

> *"The whole process of learning to arrange, for me, involved a great deal of listening to the efforts of others, plus a long history of trial and error! There's a fine line between trying to do ones best and committing emotional suicide by falling on one's own pencil, the difference being that the first idea one gets is quite often the best one, and ones which follow can sometimes be attributed to a lack of confidence in one's own efforts."*
> **Nelson Riddle** - arranger (Frank Sinatra, Rosemary Clooney, Linda Ronstadt)

Here are some arranging ideas that you can build on. These ideas can be just as easily applied to solo piano, trio, big band or orchestra and everything in between. It's also very important (and this comes back to an earlier point I made about not bullying the singer) to remember that this is a collaborative process with the vocalist. You will have lots of musical ideas to bring to the table, but leave room for the singer's vision of the song to shine through. They are the boss!

Key Changes

One of the most common arranging tricks to give a boost to the last chorus or the last 8 bars of a song, is to change key. Going up by a half-step is the usual method, (though I particularly like up a minor 3rd), and the key change is usually prepared with some sort of a ii to V movement. To prepare a key change (i.e., to play a ii-V pattern into the new key), one has to be aware of the singer's melody note and how long they might want to hold on to it! This has to be planned and decided in collaboration with the singer.

In the following example, we're coming out of the bridge of McHugh and Mercer's ballad, "Don't Blame Me." In this case, the singer, in bar 3, needs to hold onto their note for only the first two beats, leaving the last two beats for the key change. That's because the vocal G will clash badly with the Ebmi7 if it's sung all the way through the bar.

Example 1a

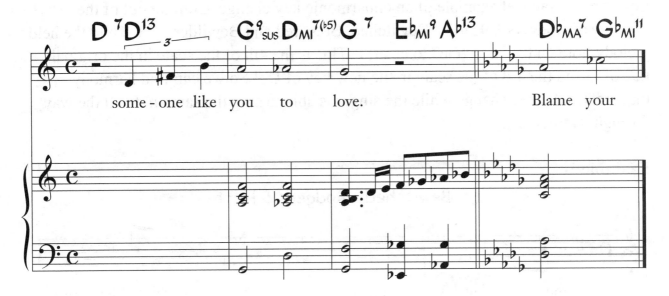

If you're lucky and find that the note the singer is holding, just before the key change, is a scale note of the new key, then a key change using that enharmonic note is possible, and sounds very smooth. First, let me explain the term enharmonic.

Enharmonic Change: "A passage in which the notation is changed, but the same keys (or notes) of the instrument are employed." The most famous example, in our music, of an enharmonic change, is the final note of the bridge of Jerome Kern's "All The Things You Are" and the first note of the last 8. The last note of the bridge is G#, the third of the key of E, and the first note of the last 8 is Ab, the minor third of Fmi7 in the new key of Ab. (See following page.)

Example 1b

All The Things You Are - Jerome Kern & Oscar Hammerstein III

Are what you are._____ Some - day my

Let's find a practical example of an enharmonic key change. Coming out of the
[55]*bridge* of Rodgers & Hart's "Bewitched, Bothered and Bewildered" we find the held
melody note on the lyric "me" to be an F. This is the 4th of the scale in the original
key of C and the 3rd of the scale in the new key of Db! So we can find harmony
that creates the key change while the singer is able to sing the same note all the way
through. Here it is…

Example 1c

Bewitched - Rodgers & Hart

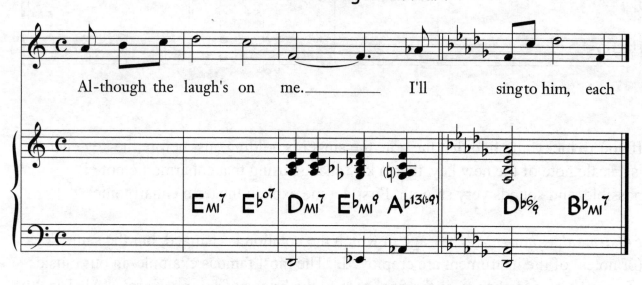

Al-though the laugh's on me._____ I'll sing to him, each

Again, the F melody note that was the 4th of the scale in C becomes the 3rd of the
scale in Db and gives us a very hip key change using Ebmi9 to Ab13 as the ii to V of
the new key.

I also like to look for unusual spots to change key, somewhere that's not obvious. The
New Yorker jazz writer, Whitney Balliett, called jazz, "The sound of surprise," and
that's what we're after with this sort of key change. As an example, in the last 8 bars
of "As Time Goes By" I change the key 2 bars into the last 8 instead of the usual spot
at the end of the bridge.

Example 1d

As Time Goes By - Herman Hupfeld

The reason this key change is possible, and reasonably easy to sing, is because we're again using an enharmonic note to get us to the next key. Enharmonic, as we've learned, means "writing the same sound in two different ways when changing from one key to another." The melody on the word "glory" in the 2nd bar of "As Time Goes By" is an F. So instead of that F being the 7th of a G7 chord, which it would be if we were staying in the key of C, it now becomes the 9th of Ebmi and the 13th of Ab7, the ii to V sequence in the new key of Db.

Over the years, dramatic key changes have become slightly cliched in pop music. Think Barry Manilow, who changed key in the last 8 bars of every song he ever sang. So be careful where and when you might use this uplifting device. But do use it!

Meter Changes - Tempo Changes

One of the magic things about the artistic independence of the jazz and cabaret worlds is that we have the freedom to interpret these songs in any way we choose. Many songs are originally from Broadway shows where they must be performed as written. We have no such restraints. We can go anywhere our imagination will take us. There's no director breathing down our necks, no orchestra playing the melody and no need for the vocalist to bellow in order to reach the last row of the balcony. So let's look at a couple of examples involving meter changes to show you what I mean.

Rodgers & Hart's lovely song "I Didn't Know What Time It Was" is written in 4/4 (Example 2a) and is usually done as a medium swing tune. I decided to leave the rarely done verse in 4/4 —but the chorus sat nicely as a jazz waltz. Example 2b is what it looks like on the page. There are two 3/4 bars for every one bar of 4/4. That means for every 2 beats in 4/4, there are 3 beats in waltz time. Here's the original for you to compare.

Example 2a

Example 2b

I often find myself taking the opposite course - changing a waltz into a 4/4 swing, especially in up-tempo numbers. Here's Lerner and Loewe's "Show Me" from "My Fair Lady". It was written as a fast waltz, and I turned it into a rousing set opener in a fast 4/4. Here's the original.

Example 2c

And here's what it became...

Example 2d

Notice that I've changed the harmony a little and used a pedal point. The original harmony of the first two bars is   C / / / | G7sus4 / / /   but in the second bar I've used a chord built on 4th's. This gives the arrangement a smooth and floating feel.

BTW, this is another of those situations where just writing the chord name on a chart probably isn't really specific enough, so I've written out, in full, the voicing that I want to hear played.

There are many options along these lines available to the imaginative arranger. It's also a common tactic to change the [56]*feel* of a song, (e.g., using a bossa nova rhythm on what's usually a swing tune, or swinging a traditional Latin song). Experiment, and see what works.

Riffs

First of all, what's a riff? In jazz, a riff is a short musical phrase that repeats. Riffs are often used as accompaniments to solos, especially in a big band setting. The early Count Basie band was famous for it's [57]*head arrangement* riffs.

Here's a piano riff that I used for Wesla Whitfield's version of "Walkin' After Midnight" from her Pismo records CD "Live at the Rrazz Room." Note that in this example the rhythmic pattern stays the same, but the notes alter in order to match the changing harmony.

Example 3a

In the trio version of this song the bass is doubling the piano's left-hand line. It's an effect that's very powerful and one that I often use.

Even though I've defined a riff as a repeated phrase, I also think of it as a generic term for written lines played in unison by the piano and bass even if they don't repeat and are more complicated. Example 3b is a be-bop style line I wrote to be played under the melody of Rodgers and Hart's "This Can't Be Love."

Example 3b

I'll often use this technique if the harmony of a song we're about to accompany is very complex, (e.g., a harmonic change on every beat in a medium tempo song, or if the melody is very chromatic and hard to harmonize without overplaying). It can be less cluttered and yet musically exciting. Think of it as a Bach two-part invention.

In the verse of "This Can't Be Love," the melody is quite chromatic. So I used a simple unison line (played with the bass) instead of trying to comp chords that might fit this meandering Richard Rodgers melody, but would restrict the vocalist's freedom to phrase across the bar line (following page).

Example 3c

Another bass and piano in unison 'riff situation' that I like to use in arrangements is what I call the "contrapuntal riff." Counterpoint can be defined as "the writing of musical lines that sound very different and move independently from each other, but sound harmonious when played simultaneously." That's exactly what we're after! In this example, the piano is playing the line in octaves and in unison with the bass.

Example 3d

You'll notice that the bass is written pretty high in it's range. I like that sound, but when arranging in this style, you need to take into account your bass player's technical ability. This is a phrase that would be played in the *[58]thumb position* on the bass. I often write lines like this in the treble clef on the bass chart, but only if the bass player is comfortable reading that clef. It saves on all those ledger lines.

Stop-Time

An effective and often used device in early jazz is stop-time. It creates tension and also includes that magic part of music, *silence*. Here are a couple of examples. In the first we'll use "Paper Moon" again.

Example 4a

It is a rare occurrence to actually see a piano part written out in full like the above chart. You're much more likely to get something like example 4b, and actually, we accompanists much prefer it! It's much less cluttered, and it gives us room to use our own chord voicings and also to alter the weight and heft of our voicings. If the passage is loud, we may play more notes and play in a more dynamic manner than if the passage is quiet and subtle when we would be much more minimalist.

Example 4b

A rhythmic pattern played in concert by the whole ensemble is a nice arranging touch. In Example 4c, in bars 1 and 2, the whole ensemble plays a rhythmic pattern under the vocal on Jerome Kern's "Bill." The rhythmic pattern builds momentum for the upcoming key change. Notice that I've used a 'non-swinging,' [59]*straight 8's,* rhythm that evokes the appropriate mood for this lovely ballad.

Example 4c

Intros and Endings

Intros

Intro is, of course, short for introduction. We need a way to get into the tune, give the vocalist their key and set an appropriate mood—whether it's just giving the singer the first note or playing 4 or 8 bars in order to set the right tempo and rhythmic feel. I must say that one of the reasons I became an arranger was because I could write a great 8 bars, a great transition, a great 4-bar ending, etc. but was often stumped by composing in longer forms. This is why I idolize all composers, especially classical composers, who are possessors of probably the greatest brains the human race has ever had to offer.

But I digress. Many of the methods for playing and harmonizing a simple introduction were covered in the chapter on solo accompaniment, but there are times when just a note to indicate the key is all that's needed. This can be achieved by sounding just a single starting note. It's sometimes safest to give the note in the correct tessitura so the vocalist doesn't suddenly start singing an octave too high! If the starting note is B below middle C, play that note. Though, conversely, an elegant way to give the starting note is by way of a "bell tone". What is a bell tone? In this context, it's usually the 5th of the key played as an octave and played higher up on the keyboard than the single note cue.

Example 5a

My wife, Wesla, often likes to sing the verse of a song *a cappella*, and if we're segueing from the previous tune, I'll quietly feed her the starting note under the applause for the previous tune. It's a wonderful effect, and invariably after a show, someone will come up and say, "That was a thrilling moment when Wesla just started singing. . . does she have perfect pitch?" Well, she doesn't but there's nothing wrong with a bit of showbiz trickery!

Introductions, when played 'in tempo,' can last as long as the arranger and singer choose. The length usually depends on the tempo. 4 bars is enough for a slow ballad, and 8 bars is just right for a medium tempo song. The musical material for the introduction can be culled from the song itself or be an original invention. As I've said before, I don't particularly like telegraphing the identity of a song by using melodic material from that song. But there are times when using the harmonic content of the last 8 bars of a song can provide a sure and safe introduction. (See "Autumn Leaves", Example 1e, in chapter 2.) You can also use just the harmonic content of the first 8 bars, and in my arrangement of Harold Arlen's "Out Of This World," that's exactly what happens. I use the same moving line, in the tenor range, that occurs in Harold Arlen's sheet music arrangement (following page).

Example 5b

This is also an arrangement that is based on a repeated riff, where the piano's left hand is again doubling the bass.

A couple of simple and effective ways to get into a tune is to have the bass play a solo intro, or the drummer pick up his brushes and play a swinging 8 bars. This tactic also introduces a new and different musical atmosphere. Remember that when you and the vocalist are putting together a show, or just a collection of songs, we're always looking to vary the colors available to us. We don't want everything to sound the same. Of course one way of introducing a tune is to have no intro at all! Just have everyone come right in. This always has a wonderfully dramatic effect.

If your vocalist can maintain good pitch, then starting the vocal [60]*a cappella* is another novel approach. Audiences invariably gasp when, after 16 bars of un-accompanied singing, the piano comes in with a rich chord and everyone is in tune!

Back in the days of the Big Bands, the orchestra would often play a whole chorus of the song before allowing the vocalist to take their turn, never mind 8 bars. But don't dismiss this idea. Everything eventually comes back in fashion!

Endings

We have to get out of this song somehow. I've found that the longer I do this, the more convinced I am there are only about four endings —plus variations thereof.

Example 6a - The rhythmic ending, descending from the flatted 5th of the key.

Example 6b - A rhythmic ending where the bass ascends in one form or another.

Example 6c - There's always the ubiquitous "Basie Ending."

Example 6d -   In ballads, finding adventurous harmony that fits the last note is fun and makes for an interesting carpet for you to improvise over while the singer holds their final note.

As always, all these decisions must be made in close collaboration with the vocalist. Some singers have great breath control and can hang on to that last note for ages. Others will need quicker and more concise endings.

All of the previous examples are what you will find in organized, written arrangements. When you're playing in less formal situations with jazz singers, you'll be called on to use your ears in deciding how to end the tune, because it all depends on what note the vocalist is sustaining. Billie Holiday loved to end a song on the ninth. Here's how I might handle that ending note if I was playing solo and had the freedom to invent the harmony on the spot. (When there's a bass player involved you don't always have that kind of freedom. You at least have to be on the same harmonic page.)

Example 6e

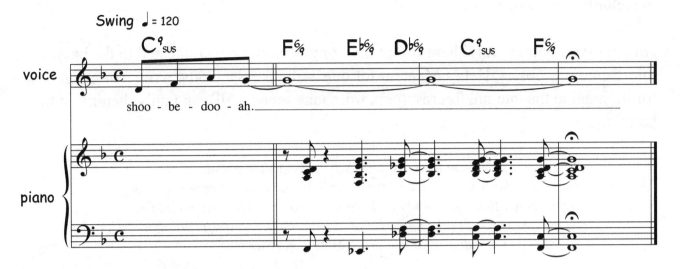

Remember that training your ear to recognize where the singer might be headed melodically is absolutely essential. Some singers will do the same thing every time in a song and others will surprise you. Which brings up an important point. An accompanist always has to be on his/her toes. If the the vocalist should omit part of the arrangement, forget lyrics, or generally mess up, you have to be there to make it all right. To make whatever sort of disaster is occurring, musical. It's no use continuing to plough through the chart if something is amiss. Use your ears! You have to make it all OK.

Re-Harmonization

What is re-harmonization? It's replacing the original harmonies of a song with chords of your own choice. It can mean changing only one chord in an 8 bar sequence, or it can mean the wholesale alteration of the composer's original intent. Starting an arrangement by referring to the original sheet music of a song (always a good idea), one will come across many levels of harmonic competence. Some composers didn't take much interest in how the song was published, so the harmony is very basic (Irving Berlin). And some were 'hands on' throughout the process and made sure that the published music contained their vision of how the song should be performed (Harold Arlen).

All jazz musicians have a love of sophisticated harmony. It's part of our DNA. But we have to be careful how we utilize this knowledge, so as not overwhelm a song or the singer with some meandering harmony that distracts from the beauty of the melody or the telling of the story.

An important point to raise here is that harmony is intimately connected to the bass line. Some composers, Henry Mancini for one, will take a melody, write a bass line for it, imagine the internal figures, (e.g., trombone section fill), and only then fill in the harmony.

> "*All chords start from the bass note. Not necessarily the tonic of the chord, but the bottom note and the notes that lead to it. They're essential. If you've got the right bass note down there, you can fool around all you want on top of it. But if your bass note's wrong, the chord isn't going to sound right no matter what you do.* " **Jimmy Rowles**

The relationship between the melody and the bass line dictates the harmony. I alway feel that the principle of the jazz approach to harmony is to use hip changes and inner lines as a sophisticated delaying tactic. We want to put off, as long as possible, arriving at the obvious harmony, like the fifth or the tonic. The simplest example of that is our creative use of the ii-V-I progression. The original sheet music of a song might look like Example 7a, a simple dominant to tonic in the key of Bb.

Example 7a

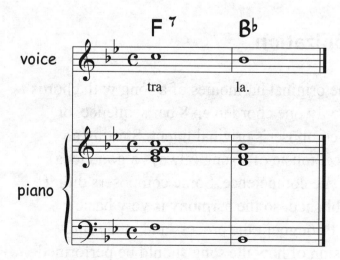

But when faced with this in a chart, we might turn it into Example 7b.

Example 7b

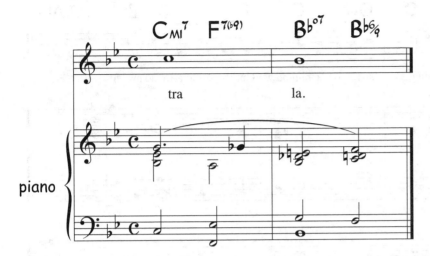

In Example 7b, we delay arriving at the F7 by inserting the Cmi7. We're coloring the F7 with a b9 and in the process we invent a nice counter melody. As an added bonus, we also delay arriving at the tonic Bb by inserting a diminished chord. This gives a feeling of suspension, until we finally arrive at the tonic Bb and find ourselves at peace with the world. (Sorry about the poetic images. It's becoming a habit.) This approach to harmony applies to our extemporized playing as well as our formal writing down of arrangements.

One of my informal mentors was the great accompanist Lou Levy, (Ella, Peggy Lee etc.). When the subject of re-harmonization came up, Lou always said that he liked to take songs apart, almost like dismantling an engine, and then put them back together again.

When arranging a standard that is in AABA format, I like to try and find different ways to harmonize each "A" section. On the following page is an example, using Harold Arlen's "I've Got The World On A String." The usual harmony is in the first example, followed by my re-harmonization of the second "A" section.

Example 7c - The original changes.

Example 7d - Re-harmonized.

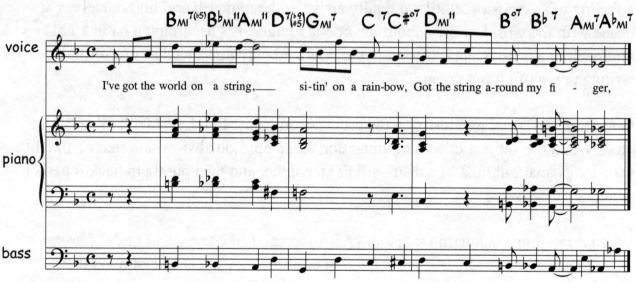

Ideas for new harmony can often come from inventing bass lines different from those in the sheet music—as long as they go with the melody! Again, the bass line dictates the harmonic content. That's what happened in the first bar of "World on a String." I found a bass line and then figured out what would sound best in terms of the quality of the chords. This is also a wonderful tactic to use when orchestrating for a large ensemble.

Bass lines are so important in many ways. As I said earlier, it's good to be able to work out arrangements from the original sheet music. But there are a few ground rules. Actually there's one ground rule: Ignore the chord symbols! Often they're ukelele chords that have little to do with real intent of the harmony. The thing to do is look at the written bass line in relation to the melody and fill out the harmony using that musical information. Whew...a little pedantic but I think I made my point.

Finally there's the complete harmonic re-invention of a passage. I did a Symphony Pops arrangement for Wesla of Harry Warren and Al Dubin's standard "September in the Rain." It is usually played as a medium swing tune and looks like this.

Example 7e

But Wesla decided she wanted to do it in a slow and atmospheric way (she has that sort of breath control), so rather than just slowing the song down and playing the written changes, I came up with a series of floating chords over a pedal point that provided the desired effect, and it looked like this:

Example 7f

I didn't indicate any chord symbols for the first two bars because these, again, are chords that need to be written out in full. They are based on intervals of a fourth with a major third perched on the top. I haven't the faintest idea what to call them, but it sounds good, and that's all that matters. A chord symbol just wouldn't fully describe what was required of the pianist.

This tune also brings up an interesting point in regard to the chord changes that jazz players like to improvise over, and it's something to keep in mind when your arrangements involve jazz solos. You can choose sophisticated harmony for backing up the vocal and then, as is often the case, simplify it for the [61]*blowing*.

In "September in the Rain," here's the changes jazzers like to play over. Compare them to the original changes in Example 7e.

Example 7g

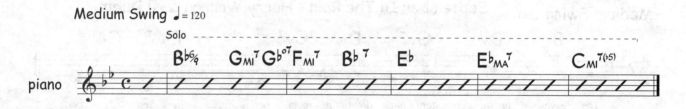

One important rule about re-harmonizing songs—You have to keep in mind that the singer may be phrasing across the bar lines. Too fussy and too busy re-harmonizing can constrict the jazz singer's freedom. You always have to think of the big picture: What tonal area are we in, and what effect will my new changes have on that picture? Often what sounds great when one is slowly working out harmony at the piano can turn into something very busy and not so great when played in tempo.

These are just a few ways to approach re-harmonization of songs, but hopefully they'll enable you to work on ideas of your own. Again, the more comprehensive your harmonic language is, the easier it is to come up with great ideas. I have to admit as I get older, the urge to write in a hip chord at every possible opportunity is fading. I'm more and more happy to comply with the composers original intent.

Medleys

Finally, a much misused tactic for arranging songs when a singer is putting together a show—the medley. A medley is a group of 2 or more songs arranged together into one piece. My wife, Wesla, has a wonderful phrase to describe medleys that have only two or three songs. She calls them "med-lets." My personal take on the medley, and remember I said this was personal, is that unless you include all of each tune in the medley, I don't want to hear it. I love these songs so much that I find it disrespectful to chop them up into pieces. Having gotten that out of my system, we'll carry on because, of course, it happens all the time.

Most of my arrangements of medleys do consist only of two or three songs. Songs might be chosen because they have the same composer and a similar lyric message. We have a medley of Irving Berlin "dance songs"Ú—"You're Easy To Dance With," "The Best Things Happen When You Dance," "It Only Happens When I Dance With You." We have quite a few that feature a ballad followed by an up-tempo, a Harry Warren medley, "I Only Have Eyes For You" and "Jeepers Creepers." Two ballads can fit well together, (e.g., "I See Your Face Before Me" and "If There Is Someone Lovelier Than You" by Arthur Schwartz and Howard Dietz). Because song titles can't be copyrighted, you can find songs of the same name. I was doing a chart on Cole Porter's "Why Shouldn't I" when I came across an Arthur Freed song called, ta-da, "Why Shouldn't I", and they fit together perfectly. I did have to make Cole Porter's "Why Shouldn't I" into a medium tempo waltz when it's usually done as a ballad, but you already know about that stuff now!

Arranging is such a large subject, (especially when it comes to orchestration), that I can't possibly cover it fully here. But once you start, you never know where you might end up—especially when the singer you're working for gets a gig with the Boston Pops, and she needs charts! So along with studying piano and 'playing for singers,' I encourage you read the great books on orchestration, Rimsky-Korsakov, Walter Piston and Samuel Adler to name just three. They will really help with your accompanying too!

Charts

Now that we have a satisfactory idea of how we're going to perform the song, let's look at how to best put it down on paper. How much information should there be on a chart? The answer is: enough so that the accompanist can make music while doing a good job of sight reading, but not so much that his head is buried in the music precluding real musical communication with the vocalist. Here's a list of minimum essentials;

1. Melody and lyrics for out-of-tempo sections - These are essential and are also recommended for the body of the song as well, if space permits. This is especially true if the song isn't well known. The inclusion of the melody gives the piano player lots of clues on how to voice chords when the song is new to him/her. And it's always useful to have the lyrics included, especially when the vocalist has a momentary lapse of memory. A whispered cue from the piano player can often save the day.

> *"I like as much information as possible to be put on a chart without it becoming confusing—certainly melody and lyric, even if it's on something in tempo. If it's a song I don't know and it's 'out of tempo', then it's essential. If I don't have a melody or a lyric, I can't do it. You can't help but freak!"*
> **Tedd Firth** (Marilyn Maye, Tom Wopat, Marlene Verplank)

2. *Clear and succinct chord changes* - We don't need a chord change on every beat unless absolutely necessary. Learn to edit yourself, and this will leave room for the accompanist's own personality to shine through.

> *"The essential harmonic information is all that's necessary. If you're in Eb, and the singer has got a B natural, Bb7(b9) will do fine. I don't need to be told about the 13, or the #5, or the b5. I'm going to figure that out. I'm gonna hear it, hear where it's going, and decide what color is best. I know the sounds."*
> **Bill Charlap**

> *"I was playing for a singer who had seemingly very nice charts but they were a damn nightmare! Every chord symbol was an experience. And if you didn't play the 13, flat 9, minus 5, plus, she would say no, no, no - no. And so you were tied in knots. So I don't like too much information about the chords. I want to voice the chords in my own way. I don't want 19 symbols."*
> **Sir Richard Rodney Bennett**

3. *All the necessary rhythmic hits* - We especially need those hits that the bass and drums are also playing. I write either just the rhythm and the chords, like this.

Example 8a

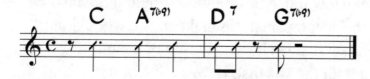

If I have specific voice leading in mind, or if the piano is doubling another instrument, I'll then write out the actual notes that I want sounded at the top of the chord, like this.

Example 8b

And if you're writing for larger ensembles the piano part often becomes a conductor/piano part. So you'll need to include all the instrumental cues as well, thus. . .

Example 8c

4. *Clear map reading* - Take time to write passages out rather than using too many repeats or multiple coda signs. Most musical train wrecks occur because of confused map reading rather than the musician's lack of sight-reading skills. You also need clear lettering or numbering so that everyone in rehearsal knows what the hell you're talking about when you say 'let's take it from letter B.' And if you've also written out a lead sheet for the vocalist make sure all the necessary information is on that part as well. On jazz charts, it's not always necessary to number each bar. Letters every 16 or 32 bars will suffice. But with charts that involve orchestras or big bands, numbering bars is highly recommended in order to save rehearsal time. Of course, all of this is a juggling act. Too many pages and page turns in a part become a problem. Bass players and drummers often have no breaks in the music in which to turn pages, so try and keep those parts to 3 pages or less. But don't make the mistake that I fell prey to occasionally in my youth. Don't have different map-reading directions on different parts. The coda needs to be in the same place on all the parts!

One of the advantages of writing on the computer is that copy and paste has made writing everything out much easier, though you will use up more paper! I have also gotten into the habit of highlighting the map-reading aspects of the chart with a red pen (e.g., the Del Segno, the Coda, the D.S. al Coda, the repeat signs and first and second time ending bars) so the road map stands out at a glance.

5. *Not too much "English" on parts* - That means not too many written out instructions. They're tough to take in when sight-reading, so try and use standard musical notation whenever possible.

Example 9a is a typical "chart" that one might encounter on an accompanying gig. It's a standard-type ballad with the first two "A" sections out-of-tempo. This chart is computer-driven (Finale), but the same principles apply to a good hand-written work. I do, however, have something to say about computer notation. I know these programs have large learning curves, but I see so many poorly-written and organized computer-driven charts. Please take the time to learn the program and apply the principles of great hand-copying. If you can locate an old copy of "The Art of Music Copying" by Clinton Roemer, buy it! Or go to the library (libraries are free!) and find "Behind Bars" by Elaine Gould, which is the current bible of music notation.

This chart starts out with a two-bar intro. Notice that this is written in full-size notation—that means we have to play those notes! Then in bars 3 thru 11, the notes are written in a smaller font to indicate they are cue notes and therefore not to be played. Under these notes are the lyric. Along with the chords, this gives us all the information we need to accompany this "out-of-tempo" passage. We need these cues in order to know where to place the accompanying chords. (Accompanying out-of-tempo or rubato passages is covered in-depth in chapter 4.) Then there are places where specific rhythms are notated (bars 16/17) but with only chords to indicate what one is expected to play. These are times when we're either playing in concert with the other musicians or the singer. The bulk of the chart is made up of chords only. This is where we really need to use our ears and concentrate on the vocalist, as well as use our good taste and experience to know where to place the chords and how to voice them. It's a ballad, so you can refer to the 'ballad comping' section of Chapter 3 for pointers on how this will be accomplished.

Now ideally, when dealing with an unfamiliar tune, we would prefer to have all the melody written out in full. But that's ideally. What we're most often faced with is exactly what we see here, a passage of chords with no indication of the melody line. So we have to fall back on our greatest asset, our ears! If you have the luxury of a rehearsal, you'll be able to get the shape of the melody in your head and be able to comp appropriately. If you don't have that luxury, then this is where your instincts, experience and good musical taste have to take over. On this chart I would still have preferred to have the melody of the bridge written out even though it's an "in tempo" part where just the chords will suffice. Note also that I only have 4 measures per line. Don't crowd the chart.

Example 9a

Piano   Wesla Whitfield

BLUE

Music - Mike Greensill   Words - Ernie Brown

Ballad ♩ = 65

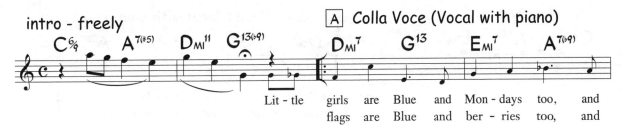

intro - freely

skies and eyes and li - lac,   lark-spur and bows and   bells and rib - bons,
jeans and jays and Vi - da,   na - vy and no - ses   Niles and notes from

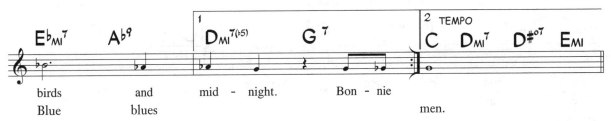

birds   and   mid - night.   Bon - nie
Blue   blues   men.

rhythm in!

Ritard ....

Colla Voce

Blue is my hea - ven,   Blue my mood and Blue   my song._____

103

Example 9b - For the curious. . . here's the complete version of "Blue."

104

There are many accompanists (myself included) who would like as much information on the chart as possible—especially if it involves an unfamiliar song. I often find that charts these days are really too minimal. But it does take a lot of effort to produce good charts, and I understand why people often take short-cuts. There are always space constraints on the chart to be taken into consideration.

There isn't room here to cover the whole world of charts from the Broadway-type Conductor/Piano scores, to Symphony Pops, to comprehensive Latin charts. But one of the questions that I put to all my famous accompanist interviewees is, "What do you look for in a great chart." There was consensus on a few points.

1. *We all hate other piano player's/arranger's changes!*

No, seriously. It's really true that for this style of playing/accompanying, we each tend to have developed a personal harmonic style that best suits our own accompanying talents. Of course, it's another "tip of the hat" to the American Popular Song that the songs can stand up to all this harmonic interference. Many accompanists work with the same vocalist on a regular basis and eventually end up playing their own charts most of the time anyway. But the lesson here is to not make your chart too complicated. Allow room for the accompanists to be themselves. Having said that, there are, of course, singers who want to hear exactly the same thing every time— especially in the show and cabaret world. So more musical detail will be needed in those charts.

2. *We don't like overly complicated chord symbols.*

They seem too anal or bossy, as though the arranger doesn't trust us to use our ears. Bill Charlap said this earlier, but it's worth repeating: "The essential information is all that's necessary. If you're in Eb and the singer has a B natural then Bb7(b9) will do fine. I don't need to be told about the 13, or the sharp 5, or the flat 5. I'm gonna figure that out. I'm going to hear it, I'm going to hear where it's going, I know the sounds. But before I dismiss it, I don't mind taking the chart home if I admire the artist and see what they're talking about and making some choices about whether or not I want to use all that information."

3.   *We really like the melody written out in full.*

Yes, I know it's a lot of work to do when often the singer can't afford even your rock-bottom arranging fee. But it will pay off in spades in performance. Especially for the piano player who doesn't know the tune.

4.   *We like the chart to be "truthful."*

What ever do I mean by truthful? Well, I don't want to deal with a situation where I have a chart in front of me, and the vocalist or [62]*M.D.* comes up to me and says, "Ignore that repeat, play this section once, and take the D.S only on the 3rd time through."

         If the arrangement has changed—WRITE IT OUT AGAIN!

I find that arranging is a wonderful and fulfilling adjunct to being an accompanist. It's an antidote to performing in front of a live audience, it is a sort of calm yin, to the tension-filled yang of having to be a perfect performer on the bandstand. And let's face it, you can go to work in your jammies.

GLOSSARY

1. *Bridge* - The middle 8 bars of a 32 bar song.

2. *Feel* - Jazz slang for the rhythmic concept of a piece.

3. *Head Arrangement* - In a jazz band, the making up riffs and backgrounds, on the spot, without the benefit of any written music. First made famous in the early Count Basie Band.

4. *Thumb Position* - The thumb position is not a traditional position, it is a stringed instrument playing technique used to facilitate playing in the upper register of the double bass, cello, and related instruments, such as the electric upright bass. To play passages in this register, the player shifts his or her hand out from behind the neck and curves the hand, using the side of the thumb to press down the string; in effect, the side of the thumb becomes a movable nut (capo). For the double bass, thumb position is used when playing above high G.

5. *Straight 8's* - Non-swinging, evenly played 8th notes. This has to be noted in jazz charts, or else there's the risk of them being played with a jazz triplet feel. Those jazzers just can't help but swing

6. *a cappella* - Italian for "in the Chapel". Designation for choral music without instrumental accompaniment. Originally the phrase referred to unaccompanied church music. Today it is used for all unaccompanied music whether sacred or secular. Even jazz musicians are allowed to use it.

7. *Blowing* - Jazz solos played over the changes.

8. *MD* - Musical Director

Chapter 6

The Accompanist as Musical Director

As we've seen, the accompanist is expected to play many musical roles above and beyond playing the piano, and he/she is often the vocalist's musical director. What does that mean? In the classical world, it describes the principle conductor. In the film world, it's the supervisor of all the music featured in the movie. On Broadway, it's the conductor who's often the rehearsal pianist as well. In our little world of jazz and cabaret, being musical director means that you're in charge of everything; at least everything that happens musically. From the hiring of the musicians, to conducting the band, from arranging the music to running a rehearsal—all on top of playing great piano accompaniment. A lot of the advice given in this chapter may seem very obvious to some, but if it can help in any way to smooth the path to better music making, it'll be worth reading.

Conducting

Orchestral and band conducting, as a musical skill, is way beyond the parameters of this book, but conducting from the piano is not. It's part of the myriad tasks that accompanists are called upon to perform. The musical arrangements we play consist of beginnings and endings, stops and starts, pauses, tempo alterations and dynamic highs and lows, all of which, in some form or other, need to be communicated to the other musicians. Most of the time, especially in a trio or duo situation, our hands will be busy. Therefore, conducting from the piano will often, by necessity, involve head nods, descriptive body language and heavy duty eye contact.

Let's talk about head nods. Head nods are usually used to denote downbeats. The dictionary tells me that a 'down beat,' two words in my dictionary, is the downward motion of the conductor's baton, marking the first beat of the measure. So our head has to substitute for the conductor's baton. Now the conductor doesn't suddenly bring the baton crashing downward. No, the conductor prepares the beat with a slight upward swoop of the hand. So this is what we must do. Lift your head slightly before bringing it down to denote the downbeat. None of these moves need to be violent or exaggerated. Your intent will come across well enough even with subtle moves, providing, of course, that the musicians can see you! Make sure you set up the bandstand so that everyone has a clear view of your head. We don't want the drummer's ride cymbal preventing him from seeing your important gestures.

The usual stage set-up for a piano trio is: the piano at stage right (BTW, you always want to have your *right hand to the audience if you can), the bass center stage, at the point of a grand piano and the drums stage left. Lately, I've been experimenting with the old Oscar Peterson stage plot of, piano at the front with the bass at the piano's left hand and the drums to the bass's left. This is best if the lid of the piano is either closed or removed, and the bass and drums are on a small riser. I like this set-up in that the bass player is physically close to my ears. I like to almost feel the bass, especially when we're trying to achieve a completely acoustic sound. As an aside on the subject of acoustic sound, I find myself having to be firm with concert hall sound engineers, asking them not to be too intrusive with their miking. My drummer, Vince Lateano, has started rebelling completely and won't let any microphones anywhere near his drum set. Bravo! Ours is a subtle art and we need to be in charge of how it sounds. I dislike microphones placed too near the piano strings—we don't listen to the piano with our ears two inches from the strings, so why would you pick up the sound to amplify in it that way? BTW that applies to recording studio work as well.

(*I've been asked why the pianist's right hand always faces the audience, and there are a couple of explanations. The lid of a grand piano opens in that direction, so therefore the audience will get the bulk of the sound. It's also a lot easier to look over my right shoulder towards the singer and the audience, as opposed to my left. It keeps the more 'active' portion of the keyboard in line with the singer. One reads music left to right so the tendency of the head is to always end up looking over the right shoulder.)

There are times, of course, when a hand or two will be free to conduct. Let's look at how to deal with a [63]*fermata*, followed by a cut-off, or as we say in the business, [64]*railroad tracks*.

Example 1

Because the Ab chord is under a fermata, we can hold that chord by using the sustain pedal on the piano and then raise the hand, palm up, to hold the fermata. This will leave our right (or left hand) free to give the cut-off. The clearest gesture when giving a cut-off is one where you move your hand a little to the left, to prepare the band, and then move it to the right while closing your fist. And then we can use our previously practiced head-nod, to give the downbeat of the *a tempo*.

When it comes to dynamics, I've found that just a slight hunching of the shoulders, while leaning forward, works well in denoting a diminuendo, and just leaning back and getting animated can encourage crescendos. Let's not forget that a lot of volume variations, especially in this small group configuration, can be conveyed by the dynamics of our own playing.

When playing a [65]*formal show,* you'll be required to set the tempos of the songs. I mentioned earlier that a silent metronome is invaluable in these situations. There are now metronomes that can be programmed to give you the tempo of each song in a show and in the order that they are to be performed!

Once we have the right tempo, how best to convey this to the musicians? In some circumstances it's just fine to audibly count off tunes. It can be part of the hip atmosphere of the show. But there are also times when it's important to be more subtle, especially in quiet and dramatic situations. I used to give the musicians an idea of the upcoming tempo by either rotating my head from side to side or by using a twisting motion in my wrist while holding up my hand. But recently (thank you Larry Dunlap), I've been using the thumb and index finger method. This is where you hold up your hand and bring the index finger down on the thumb as if you were making a talking motion, think shadow puppets. The advantage of this method, other than being quiet, is that the tapping of the index finger on the thumb gives a very precise idea of where the beat falls. These silent methods of signaling a tempo enable you to start the next tune or section with only a nod of your head for a down beat instead of a prolonged and audible count in. And that's because the musicians will now have the tempo you want clearly in their heads.

Conducting large ensembles from the piano can be done, but it is tough to do—mainly because it's hard for you to be clearly seen by every section of the orchestra. And, of course, you are busy accompanying at the piano. When I'm playing a symphony pops date, and I'm arranging the music, I will often tailor the arrangements so that most of the tempos are set by my piano introductions. This a very useful tactic if you are attempting to conduct from the piano, but is also useful even if there is a real conductor present. Because then, the conductor doesn't have to memorize your vocalist's tempos! Of course, with an orchestra at your disposal, the need for piano accompaniment is diminished. You can use the orchestra as accompanist. Therefore you are free to conduct from the piano, and free to stand up when it's necessary to be seen by the 4th trombonist. That is, as long as your knees are in good shape, and you don't mind all that bouncing up and down.

Rehearsals

First, let's look at the times when it's just you and the vocalist getting things together. These rehearsals are not only the opportunity to practice the music, but a time to bond both musically and personally, and to get a sense of the artist with whom you'll be working.

> *"You need a good marriage with a singer. I'll know within 16 bars whether we're going to be married or not. It's a mysterious thing, isn't it?"* - **George Shearing**
> (Mel Torme, Carmen McCrae - quoted in "Jazz Voices"
> by Kitty Grime - Quartet Books)

If it's a singer who's new to you, try to get the charts ahead of time so that you can be well-prepared. If it's a session to discover new tunes and experiment with arrangements, bring your own thoughts and suggestions. The singer will appreciate that you care and want to get involved in the creative process. You aren't just a piano player for hire.

> *"I'm not an accompanist. I don't like the word 'accompanying.' I'm 'collaborating,' that's more my thing. I don't think I'm just an accompanist that you wheel on to play for singers. I'm collaborating with the singer."*
> **Sir Richard Rodney Bennett.**

This next section means no disrespect to those many highly trained singers with BA's in music. On occasion, a vocalist may express their song ideas in language not strictly musical, but in a more emotional and impressionistic manner. It's your job to interpret the vocalist's vision and translate it into practical musical ideas. If the lyric of a passage expresses yearning, don't suggest a perky two-beat rhythm. Pay attention to all aspects of the song; it's mood, lyric intent, harmonic complexity, melodic arc, etc.

Of course, you hope that the singer is also well-prepared when coming to rehearsal. But oft times they are not, and they are using you to learn the material. This is okay if you're being paid for your time. But if you're doing an unpaid rehearsal for an upcoming gig, it's not okay. When dealing with a young/inexperienced vocalist who's not prepared, this is the time to (subtly and nicely) advise them of the advantages of learning to read music and learning to play some basic piano. By doing so, they can come to rehearsal fully prepared. You can also tell them that this is a wonderful way to discover new repertoire (playing through piles of old sheet music is always exciting) and to even get into the scary world of writing your own original material. Every musician and singer should play some [66]*arranger's piano.*

> *"I used to play piano and that's how I taught myself to sing. I get the music, and I learn the song. I don't listen to no records."* **Helen Humes**
> (quoted in "Jazz Voices" by Kitty Grime - Quartet Books)

> *"Mabel Mercer would work on her songs by constantly going over them, over and over and over. I hated to go to rehearsal with her, because we'd do one song all day! "* **Jimmy Lyon** (June Christy, Mabel Mercer)

Rehearsals are when those transposing skills you've been working on can really come to the fore. As I've said, some vocalists will come to rehearsals completely prepared with keys and arrangements already decided upon. But often rehearsals are when the vocalist wants to experiment and see where a certain song might fit in their voice. If the song is not too complex, or it's a familiar tune, using our ears and learned transposing skills will suffice. But I've found in these situations that if a song is a little complicated, or the new key is a little esoteric, there's nothing wrong with taking time out to sketch out the harmonic outline of the new key. It's much better than floundering away in strange waters. BTW, always bring a pencil to rehearsal, and have some blank manuscript at hand. You never know when you might need to make notes on the charts, or need to quickly sketch out a riff for the bass player.

While we're in the 'advice to vocalists department' (remember to always be diplomatic), I have a few pet peeves I thought I'd share with you. One is how charts are presented to me at the piano. I know that keeping music, between plastic, in a ring binder is a convenient way for the vocalist to carry around their repertoire, but it's a pain in the neck to read. The light reflects off the plastic, and it's hard to turn pages quickly and accurately.

Another complaint is charts that aren't taped together and are printed on flimsy bits of regular copy paper. They continually blow off/fall off the piano desk. Try to get your singer to use heavier stock and at least tape the pages together in booklet form. That's done by laying down the first two pages and taping them, then turning them over, adding the third page which will be taped on the backside etc. etc. to form a booklet that will open like an accordion.

I have to admit that I'm guilty of using letter size paper for my parts these days, but I'm not proud of it. I long for the days of real manuscript, size 9 ½ by 12 ½, and I'm saving my pennies for a large format printer!

In the professional world, so many of our rehearsals are combined with a soundcheck in the hours before the actual show. Let's imagine that we have a trio gig, backing up a vocalist in concert. Soundcheck is when we usually get to rehearse with the bass and drums. Time is always at a premium, and efficiency is our watchword.

> *We all hate to be lectured to, BUT the number one rule for the professional musician is to be on time! You wouldn't think of casually getting to the actual show 10 minutes after curtain time, so why are so many musicians late for rehearsals? Get's me.*

It's in these rehearsals where your careful preparation will pay off. The charts are in order and opened. You have clear, easily readable rehearsal markings on the charts so that the musicians will know where they are at any given time. The tempos of the songs are firmly in your brain, or the metronome. If segues aren't marked on the charts, this is the time to warn the band when they might occur, so that they can be prepared for a quick downbeat. If the material is familiar or reasonably easy, there's often no need to rehearse songs all the way through, just beginnings and endings. I like to leave some surprises for the musicians, and often the vocalist doesn't want to sing all out. (I'm superstitious about really good rehearsals. I want to save inspiration for the show. I love good rehearsals, but when they aren't on a 'show day.')

Soundcheck/rehearsals can be problematic because you're trying to accomplish two things at once; rehearse the band, and get the sound just right so that everyone can hear what they need to hear. I find that there are two ways one can approach this problem:

1. Let the sound guy do his thing around you and ignore him while you rehearse.
2. Get the sound right and then rehearse. There's nothing worse than rehearsals being interrupted by musicians whining for "more bass in my monitor."

Sometimes you'll be called on to run the rehearsal without the singer being present. In this situation, it's very helpful if you can, vocally or instrumentally, approximate the vocal lines so that the band has an idea of what they will hear during the performance.

Shows

There are usually two sorts of shows involving singers; those that are quite formal in [67]*listening situations,* such as cabarets, good jazz clubs and concert stages, and those that are loose and informal, such as a club or a bar. As we've seen in the rehearsal section, I tend to be picky about how formal shows are run and expect, for example, that the musician's charts be fully opened and in order. There's nothing more annoying than the crackling sound of charts being opened while the singer is telling a poignant story about the loss of a favorite cat. The more relaxed bar/club show is where tunes are often called on the bandstand, rather than being rehearsed and decided on beforehand. I find it strange to have written the word 'relaxed' in the last sentence. I'm one of those musicians who's more comfortable and relaxed when I know what's going to happen in advance, and I've been able to prepare. But the professional accompanist must be prepared for all these circumstances.

If it's a formal show, make sure that all the musicians have a set list. That way they can always be sure that their music is in the right order without having to run and ask you! Make sure you include [68]*tacet sheets* when there's a song in the set without a chart. Make sure you know when the vocalist wants to talk between songs, and therefore, which songs are to be segues. These 'tactics' will usually be decided by the vocalist when putting the show together. But there are many times when a set list will be thrust into your hand a minute or so before showtime. This is, of course, another reason to make sure that all musician's charts are open. Then they're ready to start the next tune whenever you should give the downbeat.

Again, make sure you know all of the song tempos in the show, especially in the case of segues. You don't want to be wracking your brains for the right tempo of the next song—especially during that awkward moment of silence when the applause from the previous tune has sputtered out. If you have a hard time remembering tempos, we did talk about the efficacy of a good, silent metronome, although I think it's very useful to try and memorize certain metronome markings and get them permanently into your head. For example; a lot of medium swing tunes seem to fall into the 120 [69]*b.m.p.* category, and I remember that tempo by using a tune I know well as a [70]*mnemonic* device. In the case of 120 b.p.m, I think of the tempo of Duke Ellington's song, "In a

Mellow Tone." It always seems to come out right. A ballad at 60 b.m.p. is easy; count one thousand, two thousand, three thousand etc. and you'll be fairly accurate. All the other tempos will come with practice, so find your own mnemonics—love that word.

Often young, inexperienced singers don't have the skill-set to put together a cogent show. There are too many ballads, too many up-tempos, nothing romantic, nothing funny etc. The accompanist should be able to help with this task. Study set lists from successful singers you've played for, remember what works and what doesn't. Remember how the audience reacts to certain tempos and moods. Remember to be diplomatic with the singer. Help and advise, but don't bully!

Let me give you some ideas. Here's a typical set list for one of Wesla Whitfield's shows. Remember this is a very personal way of composing a set list, there are countless permutations available to you. This is a typical nightclub set for us, a one hour and twenty minute show with no intermission.

Overture - Trio instrumental - Lively
1. My Shining Hour (Arlen/Mercer) - Ballad - C
2. He Loves Me (Harnick/Bock) - Up-Tempo Opener - C
3. Let There Be Love (Grant/Rand) - Medium Tempo - Ab
4. Someone To Watch Over Me (Gershwins) - Ballad - G
5. Come To The Supermarket (Cole Porter) - Up-Tempo and Funny - Cm
6. At Long Last Love (Cole Porter) - Medium Swing list song - F
7. Blues Are Brewin' (Alter/De Lange) - Bluesy Medium - G
8. I Didn't Know What Time It Was (Rodgers and Hart) - Up Jazz Waltz - C
9. Mike Greensill Trio Instrumental/Vocal
10. Let's Get Away From It All (Adair/Dennis) - Medium Vocal Duet w. MG - Bb
11. Love Letters (Young/Heyman) - Ballad - Eb
12. Just In Time (Styne/Cahn) - Medium Swing - Bass & Vocal - F
13. Happy As The Day Is Long (Arlen/Koehler) - Up-Tempo Romp - F
14. I Never Has Seen Snow (Arlen Capote) - Tragic Ballad - C
15. Cheek to Cheek (Irving Berlin) - Up-Tempo Closer - F
16. In My Life (Lennon/McCartney) - Big Ballad Encore - Db

First thing to notice is that Wesla always opens with a ballad. It's always a short, succinct ballad and an optimistic one. . .no tragedy at the start of the show. Opening with a ballad isn't a normal approach, but it works well to capture the audience's attention. It also works because the playing of a lively instrumental overture sets it up.

> *"Billie Holiday would do it, go out there and start with something real soft and pretty, you know. And surprise them."* **Jimmy Rowles**
> (quoted in "Jazz Voices" by Kitty Grime - Quartet Books)

> *"One thing I did learn early on, mainly in the northern English clubs, was that if you sang a rip-roaring, grab their attention-type songs, well, you didn't grab them. Because they were so used to them, they'd talk through them, and drink through them. But if you started with a song that was low-key, they'd suddenly wonder what you were doing up there, not singing. I found the less you yelled, the more attention you got."* **Cleo Laine**
> (quoted in "Jazz Voices" by Kitty Grime - Quartet Books)

After the opening ballad, we segue into the 'traditional' up-tempo opener, and after that Wesla will talk to the audience. Wesla dislikes the term 'patter' that's often used for the talking portion of a nightclub act. She thinks it's a demeaning term for what is actually intelligent, often funny and carefully planned, dialogue.

The first two tunes don't usually include any instrumental passages. We want to feature the singer. The third tune, "Let There Be Love," is a relaxed swinger, with an [71]*a cappella* verse, and the first chorus is a duet with vocal and bass—remember, we're always looking to vary the colors and moods of a performance.

The fourth tune is a formulaic thing for us. We always try to do a very well-known ballad in this spot. It relaxes the audience. You can hear them sigh with satisfaction and say to themselves, "I think I'm going to like this."

Then we'll segue into another up-tempo, a funny and obscure Cole Porter list song titled "Come To The Supermarket." We'll follow it up in the 6th spot with another Porter list song. It's a swinger called "At Long Last Love," which will include some instrumental jazz choruses.

*Regarding instrumental interludes, there are many ways of dealing
with this sometimes contentious subject. If you're on a pure jazz gig
with an out-and-out jazz singer, you may get to solo on every tune! If
you're in a cabaret setting, you may only solo sparingly, if at all.*

*I do remember hearing Carmen McCrae live many times. She would
very rarely give a piano solo during her show and she's certainly
a bona fide jazz singer. But Carmen was the the show! So if you're
helping organize the show, pick your solo spots carefully, and balance
the program. Acquire some showbiz savvy!*

You'll notice on the set list, I've included the keys of the songs. You don't want too
many songs in a row in the same key. It's sounds dull, especially to the musicians.

*"We have a sort of format that we've evolved over the years,
although the songs change, of course. We figure out tunes that follow
each other gracefully, different tempos, different keys. It bugs me to
play 3 songs in a row in the same key."* **Roy Kral**
(Jackie and Roy vocal duo)

#7 "Blues are Brewing" is a bluesy ballad, and #8 is 'I Didn't Know What Time It
Was," a jazz waltz. We have achieved much variety so far, in tempo and mood. Now,
at number 9, it's time for the spotlight to fall on the band. This is a recent innovation,
but Wesla now feels (Shhhh….) that she likes to rest the vocal chords for a tune in the
middle of the show.

Also new to our shows at #10, is a duet. I got so many requests to sing that I finally
gave in, and people seem to love the romantic duet. (Lesson #1: don't give up on your
voice. Another string to the bow never hurts.)

It's now time for another ballad. All of us adore ballads, but you can't do 16 ballads
in a row and expect the audience to stay awake. They have to be cleverly dispersed
among all the other tempos and moods. This ballad, #11 "Love Letters," is a
wonderful Victor Young song that's usually a medium tempo. But we do it very
slowly. That's followed by a vocal and bass duet on Jule Styne and Sammy Cahn's
swinger, #12, "Just In Time."

Lucky #13, "Happy As The Day Is Long," is a Harold Arlen romp that he and Ted
Koehler wrote for the Cotton Club Revue. This one features everybody in the trio.

Then at last we come to the dramatic ballad, a favorite spot in the show. This time we stay with Harold Arlen ('same composer' sections are always a good idea) and feature a wonderful song from his show "House of Flowers," a show he co-wrote with author Truman Capote. #14, "I Never Has Seen Snow."

Finally, we come to #15, the rousing closer, Irving Berlin's wonderful Fred and Ginger dance number, "Cheek To Cheek." Wesla always announces that this will be followed with the encore whether you applaud or not! It saves all that running off the stage and hoping that they applaud long enough for you to get back on. The encore in this show is the Lennon and McCartney masterpiece "In My Life," sure to send the audience out with a tear in the eye.

An obvious, but often forgotten piece of business at this stage of the show, is the play-off. After the rousing closer, I'll play a snippet of up-tempo blues under the applause. It encourages the audience! And after the encore, we'll play an extended blues until Wesla has left the stage and they've stop applauding. Show over.

Some practical considerations—if the singer has a new album, the last song of the set, at the least, should be from that CD. The audience will always ask, "Have you recorded that last song we heard?" For years we did it it the wrong way round. We would perform songs for a year until we perfected them and knew them inside out. Then we'd record them, and then we'd never do them again! Wrong! It made for great recordings but uncertain sales.

Hiring and Firing

I'm not going to say a lot on this subject. Some things just have to be learned through bitter experience. But what I will say (and it maybe so obvious that it's redundant) is always hire the very best musicians. The music will sound better. You'll learn a vast amount from musicians more experienced than you, and most of all, you'll personally play better! I have found that when you have complete confidence in your bandmates, it's much easier to play well. It's easier to play less. I often play my worst when I'm trying to cover up for a less than stellar rhythm section, or when I'm trying help a struggling singer to hit the right notes. In those circumstances, it's so easy to overplay and lose, what I know, is my innate good taste.

Well, now you have a modicum of knowledge about the art of accompaniment. Take it out into the world and make some magnificent music. Good Luck!

GLOSSARY

1. Fermata - A fermata (also known as a hold, pause, colloquially a birdseye or cyclops eye, or as a grand pause when placed over a bar—usual abbreviation is GP) is an element of musical notation indicating that the note should be sustained for longer than its note value would indicate. Exactly how much longer it is held is up to the discretion of the performer or conductor, but twice as long is not unusual. It is usually printed above, but occasionally below (upside down), the note that is to be held longer. Occasionally, holds are also printed above rests or barlines, indicating a pause of indefinite duration.

2. Railroad Tracks - The real name should be *Caesura*. In musical notation, caesura denotes a brief, silent pause, during which metrical time is not counted. Similar to a silent fermata, caesuras are located between notes or measures (before or over barlines), rather than on notes or rests (as with a fermata). A fermata may be placed over a caesura to indicate a longer pause. In musical notation, the symbol for a caesura is a pair of parallel lines set at an angle, rather like a pair of forward slashes: //. The symbol is popularly called "tram-lines" in the U.K. and "railroad tracks" in the U.S.

3. Formal Show - A formal show is when a pre-planned set list is used, and songs are either segued from one to the other, or the artist engages in amusing patter. It's the opposite of your usual fall-about, 'what the hell shall we play next,' jazz club set. Of course, there are gradations of formal shows; from the tightly scripted musical to the looser cabaret performance with the common denominator being an attentive and quiet audience.

4. Arranger's Piano - Enough basic keyboard knowledge to allow one to work out melodies, voicings and arranging ideas at the piano.

5. Listening Situations - The audience is quiet, as in a theater, and everyone has specifically come to hear the performance.

6. Tacet Sheet - A blank piece of paper with the title of the song to be performed. This way musicians, without charts for a particular song, will still know where they are in the show.

7. BPM - Beats per minute. Denoting the tempo of the song.

8. Mnemonic - A mnemonic (pronounced with a silent "m"), or mnemonic device, is any learning technique that aids information retention. Mnemonics aim to translate information into a form that the human brain can retain better than its original form. Even the process of applying this conversion might already aid the transfer of information to long-term memory. Commonly encountered mnemonics are often for lists and in auditory form, such as short poems, acronims, or memorable phrases, but mnemonics can also be for other types of information and in visual or kinesthetic forms. Their use is based on the observation that the human mind more easily remembers spatial, personal, surprising, physical, sexual, humorous, or otherwise 'relatable' information, rather than more abstract or impersonal forms of information.

9. a cappella - Officially this is defined as "In the church or chapel style, that is, vocal music, unaccompanied." But it's certainly come to mean any unaccompanied singing.

Thanks and Acknowledgements

First of all, thanks and much love to my wonderful wife and superb editor, vocalist Wesla Whitfield. Wesla taught me to revere and respect the story-telling in songs as much as the music, and that knowledge is so essential to great accompanying.

This book would not have even gotten off the ground without the aid my pal Barry Sinclair. His computer and internet savvy, along with his superb artistic sensibility and design skills, have been essential to my work—and Barry is responsible for the cover art.

Next, thanks to all the "Kickstarter" contributors (you know who you are) without whose support I would never have been able to set aside the time to write this book.

The knowledge imparted by all of you fabulous accompanists I had the pleasure of interviewing was invaluable in organizing my thoughts, and all your quotes were perfect. Thanks, Bill Charlap, Christian Jacob, Tedd Firth, Sir Richard Rodney Bennett, Lee Musiker, Christopher Denny, John McDaniel, George Mesterhazy, David Newton and Larry Dunlap. I'd also like to thank maestro Mike Renzi for his warm and succinct whispering in my ears over the years, invaluable advice for the budding accompanist. And especially, thanks to all the great accompanists I've listened to down the years who were such an inspiration to me: Jimmy Rowles, Tommy Flanagan, Norman Simmons, Ellis Larkins, Lou Levy, Teddy Wilson, George Shearing, Kenny Barron…the list goes on and on!

Thanks to singers Madeline Eastman, Marylin Maye and Maye Cavallero for their thoughts and to all the wonderful singers I've played for over the years, they taught me well. And, of course, my own stellar rhythm section, John Wiitala on bass and Vince Lateano on drums.

Many thanks to my publisher, Chuck Sher, and my musical editor, Larry Dunlap.

About Mike Greensill…

After graduating in 1972 from Leeds College of Music in England, Mike toured Europe and the Far East and lived in Hong Kong for 4 years before finally settling into his adopted home, San Francisco, in 1977. Mike and his wife, vocalist Wesla Whitfield, moved to St. Helena in Napa Valley in 2006.

Mike is well-known for his role as musical director to acclaimed vocalist Wesla Whitfield with whom he has recorded twenty albums. Mike is also the resident piano player on Sedge Thomson's weekly Public Radio show, "West Coast Live"—more info at wcl.org. Mike can also be caught playing jazz with his trio in many a Bay Area concert hall and jazz club.

As an arranger, in addition to his work with Wesla, Mike has had the opportunity to write for big bands and symphony orchestras, including commissions from the Boston Pops, the San Francisco Symphony and the Buffalo Philharmonic Orchestra.

Mike has also had the pleasure of accompanying such diverse talents as Rita Moreno and Margaret Whiting, Broadway stars Lillias White and Franc D'Ambrosio and jazz singers Madeline Eastman, Denise Perrier, Ann Hampton Callaway and Cheryl Bentine from the Manhattan Transfer..

Mike's latest CD, The Mike Greensill Trio "Live at the Plush Room," is available online at CD Baby and Amazon.com. His writing and arranging for the Kronos Quartet can be found on Wesla Whitfield's HighNote Records CD, "September Songs." Wesla's CD "Livin' on Love" also on HighNote Records, features Mike's arrangements for The Klingel Horns, a french horn quartet lead by SF Opera's principle Horn Bill Klingelhoffer. To hear some of Mike's arranging and read his scores go to www.mikegreensill.com and click on arranging/orchestration.

"Greensill is an accompanist in the great tradition of Jimmy Rowles and Ellis Larkins.
It's worth twice the price of admission just to hear him!" - Terry Teachout - NY Daily News

The San Francisco Chronicle's Jesse Hamlin calls Greensill - *"The perfect accompanist."*

Phillip Elwood, jazz critic at the San Francisco Examiner
"Greensill is a wonderful jazz pianist."

www.mikegreensill.com   E-mail - mike@mikegreensill.com

SHER MUSIC CO. – *The finest in Jazz & Latin Publications*

THE NEW REAL BOOK SERIES

The Standards Real Book (C, Bb or Eb)

A Beautiful Friendship	Days Of Wine And Roses	I Only Have Eyes For You	Old Folks	Summer Night
A Time For Love	Dreamsville	I'm A Fool To Want You	On A Clear Day	Summertime
Ain't No Sunshine	Easy To Love	Indian Summer	Our Love Is Here To Stay	Teach Me Tonight
Alice In Wonderland	Embraceable You	It Ain't Necessarily So	'Round Midnight	That Sunday, That Summer
All Of You	Falling In Love With Love	It Never Entered My Mind	Secret Love	The Girl From Ipanema
Alone Together	From This Moment On	It's You Or No One	September In The Rain	Then I'll Be Tired Of You
At Last	Give Me The Simple Life	Just One Of Those Things	Serenade In Blue	There's No You
Baltimore Oriole	Have You Met Miss Jones?	Love For Sale	Shiny Stockings	Time On My Hands
Bess, You Is My Woman	Hey There	Lover, Come Back To Me	Since I Fell For You	'Tis Autumn
Bluesette	I Can't Get Started	The Man I Love	So In Love	Where Or When
But Not For Me	I Concentrate On You	Mr. Lucky	So Nice (Summer Samba)	Who Cares?
Close Enough For Love	I Cover The Waterfront	My Funny Valentine	Some Other Time	With A Song In My Heart
Crazy He Calls Me	I Love You	My Heart Stood Still	Stormy Weather	You Go To My Head
Dancing In The Dark	I Loves You Porgy	My Man's Gone Now	The Summer Knows	**And Hundreds More!**

The New Real Book - Volume 1 (C, Bb or Eb)

Angel Eyes	Eighty One	I Thought About You	My Shining Hour	Shaker Song
Anthropology	E.S.P.	If I Were A Bell	Nature Boy	Skylark
Autumn Leaves	Everything Happens To Me	Imagination	Nefertiti	A Sleepin' Bee
Beautiful Love	Feel Like Makin' Love	The Island	Nothing Personal	Solar
Bernie's Tune	Footprints	Jersey Bounce	Oleo	Speak No Evil
Blue Bossa	Four	Joshua	Once I Loved	St. Thomas
Blue Daniel	Four On Six	Lady Bird	Out Of This World	Street Life
But Beautiful	Gee Baby Ain't I Good	Like Someone In Love	Pent Up House	Tenderly
Chain Of Fools	To You	Little Sunflower	Portrait Of Tracy	These Foolish Things
Chelsea Bridge	Gone With The Wind	Lush Life	Put It Where You Want It	This Masquerade
Compared To What	Here's That Rainy Day	Mercy, Mercy, Mercy	Robbin's Nest	Three Views Of A Secret
Darn That Dream	I Love Lucy	The Midnight Sun	Ruby, My Dear	Waltz For Debby
Desafinado	I Mean You	Monk's Mood	Satin Doll	Willow Weep For Me
Early Autumn	I Should Care	Moonlight In Vermont	Search For Peace	**And Many More!**

The New Real Book Play-Along CDs (For Volume 1)

CD #1 - Jazz Classics - Lady Bird, Bouncin' With Bud, Up Jumped Spring, Monk's Mood, Doors, Very Early, Eighty One, Voyage **& More!**
CD #2 - Choice Standards - Beautiful Love, Darn That Dream, Moonlight In Vermont, Trieste, My Shining Hour, I Should Care **& More!**
CD #3 - Pop-Fusion - Morning Dance, Nothing Personal, La Samba, Hideaway, This Masquerade, Three Views Of A Secret, Rio **& More!**
World-Class Rhythm Sections, featuring Mark Levine, Larry Dunlap, Sky Evergreen, Bob Magnusson, Keith Jones, Vince Lateano & Tom Hayashi

The New Real Book - Volume 2 (C, Bb or Eb)

Afro-Centric	Django	I'm Glad There Is You	Nica's Dream	Stablemates
After You've Gone	Equinox	Impressions	Once In A While	Stardust
Along Came Betty	Exactly Like You	In Your Own Sweet Way	Perdido	Sweet And Lovely
Bessie's Blues	Falling Grace	It's The Talk Of The Town	Rosetta	That's All
Black Coffee	Five Hundred Miles High	Jordu	Sea Journey	There Is No Greater Love
Blues For Alice	Freedom Jazz Dance	Killer Joe	Senor Blues	'Til There Was You
Body And Soul	Giant Steps	Lullaby Of The Leaves	September Song	Time Remembered
Bolivia	Harlem Nocturne	Manha De Carnaval	Seven Steps To Heaven	Turn Out The Stars
The Boy Next Door	Hi-Fly	The Masquerade Is Over	Silver's Serenade	Unforgettable
Bye Bye Blackbird	Honeysuckle Rose	Memories Of You	So Many Stars	While We're Young
Cherokee	I Hadn't Anyone 'Til You	Moment's Notice	Some Other Blues	Whisper Not
A Child Is Born	I'll Be Around	Mood Indigo	Song For My Father	Will You Still Be Mine?
Cold Duck Time	I'll Get By	My Ship	Sophisticated Lady	You're Everything
Day By Day	Ill Wind	Naima	Spain	**And Many More!**

The New Real Book - Volume 3 (C, Bb, Eb or Bass clef)

Actual Proof	Dolphin Dance	I Hear A Rhapsody	Maiden Voyage	Speak Like A Child
Ain't That Peculair	Don't Be That Way	If You Could See Me Now	Moon And Sand	Spring Is Here
Almost Like Being In Love	Don't Blame Me	In A Mellow Tone	Moonglow	Stairway To The Stars
Another Star	Emily	In A Sentimental Mood	My Girl	Star Eyes
Autumn Serenade	Everything I Have Is Yours	Inner Urge	On Green Dolphin Street	Stars Fell On Alabama
Bird Of Beauty	For All We Know	Invitation	Over The Rainbow	Stompin' At The Savoy
Black Nile	Freedomland	The Jitterbug Waltz	Prelude To A Kiss	Sweet Lorraine
Blue Moon	The Gentle Rain	Just Friends	Respect	Taking A Chance On Love
Butterfly	Get Ready	Just You, Just Me	Ruby	This Is New
Caravan	A Ghost Of A Chance	Knock On Wood	The Second Time Around	Too High
Ceora	Heat Wave	The Lamp Is Low	Serenata	(Used To Be A) Cha Cha
Close Your Eyes	How Sweet It Is	Laura	The Shadow Of Your Smile	When Lights Are Low
Creepin'	I Fall In Love Too Easily	Let's Stay Together	So Near, So Far	You Must Believe In Spring
Day Dream	I Got It Bad	Lonely Woman	Solitude	**And Many More!**

The All Jazz Real Book

Over 540 pages of tunes as recorded by: Miles, Trane, Bill Evans, Cannonball, Scofield, Brecker, Yellowjackets, Bird, Mulgrew Miller, Kenny Werner, MJQ, McCoy Tyner, Kurt Elling, Brad Mehldau, Don Grolnick, Kenny Garrett, Patitucci, Jerry Bergonzi, Stanley Clarke, Tom Harrell, Herbie Hancock, Horace Silver, Stan Getz, Sonny Rollins, and MORE!

Includes a free CD of many of the melodies (featuring Bob Sheppard & Friends.). $44 list price. Available in C, Bb, Eb

The European Real Book

An amazing collection of some of the greatest jazz compositions ever recorded! Available in C, Bb and Eb. $40

- Over 100 of Europe's best jazz writers.
- 100% accurate, composer-approved charts.
- 400 pages of fresh, exciting sounds from virtually every country in Europe.
- Sher Music's superior legibility and signature calligraphy makes reading the music easy.

Listen to FREE MP3 FILES of many of the songs at **www.shermusic.com!**

See **www.shermusic.com** for more information, including a complete list of tunes in all our fake books.

To order, call (800) 444-7437 or fax (707) 763-2038

SHER MUSIC JAZZ PUBLICATIONS

The Real Easy Book Vol. 1
TUNES FOR BEGINNING IMPROVISERS

Published by Sher Music Co. in conjunction with the Stanford Jazz Workshop. $22 list price.

The easiest tunes from Horace Silver, Eddie Harris, Freddie Hubbard, Red Garland, Sonny Rollins, Cedar Walton, Wes Montgomery Cannonball Adderly, etc. Get yourself or your beginning jazz combo sounding good right away with the first fake book ever designed for the beginning improviser.
Available in C, Bb, Eb and Bass Clef.

The Real Easy Book Vol. 2
TUNES FOR INTERMEDIATE IMPROVISERS

Published by Sher Music Co. in conjunction with the Stanford Jazz Workshop. Over 240 pages. $29.

The best intermediate-level tunes by: Charlie Parker, John Coltrane, Miles Davis, John Scofield, Sonny Rollins, Horace Silver, Wes Montgomery, Freddie Hubbard, Cal Tjader, Cannonball Adderly, and more! Both volumes feature instructional material tailored for each tune. Perfect for jazz combos!
Available in C, Bb, Eb and Bass Clef.

The Real Easy Book Vol. 3
A SHORT HISTORY OF JAZZ

Published by Sher Music Co. in conjunction with the Stanford Jazz Workshop. Over 200 pages. $25.

History text and tunes from all eras and styles of jazz. Perfect for classroom use. Available in C, Bb, Eb and Bass Clef versions.

The Best of Sher Music Co. Real Books
100+ TUNES YOU NEED TO KNOW

A collection of the best-known songs from the world leader in jazz fake books – Sher Music Co.!

Includes songs by: Miles Davis, John Coltrane, Bill Evans, Duke Ellington, Antonio Carlos Jobim, Charlie Parker, John Scofield, Michael Brecker, Weather Report, Horace Silver, Freddie Hubbard, Thelonious Monk, Cannonball Adderley, and many more!
$26. Available in C, Bb, Eb and Bass Clef.

The Serious Jazz Book II
THE HARMONIC APPROACH

By Barry Finnerty, Endorsed by: Joe Lovano, Jamey Aebersold, Hubert Laws, Mark Levine, etc.

- A 200 page, exhaustive study of how to master the harmonic content of songs.
- Contains explanations of every possible type of chord that is used in jazz.
- Clear musical examples to help achieve real harmonic control over melodic improvisation.
- For any instrument. $32. Money back gurantee!

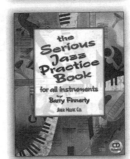

The Serious Jazz Practice Book By Barry Finnerty

A unique and comprehensive plan for mastering the basic building blocks of the jazz language. It takes the most widely-used scales and chords and gives you step-by-step exercises that dissect them into hundreds of cool, useable patterns.
Includes CD - $30 list price.

"The book I've been waiting for!" – Randy Brecker.

"The best book of intervallic studies I've ever seen."
– Mark Levine

The Jazz Theory Book

By Mark Levine, the most comprehensive Jazz Theory book ever published! $38 list price.

- Over 500 pages of text and over 750 musical examples.
- Written in the language of the working jazz musician, this book is easy to read and user-friendly. At the same time, it is the most comprehensive study of jazz harmony and theory ever published.
- Mark Levine has worked with Bobby Hutcherson, Cal Tjader, Joe Henderson, Woody Shaw, and many other jazz greats.

Jazz Piano Masterclass With Mark Levine "THE DROP 2 BOOK"

The long-awaited book from the author of "The Jazz Piano Book!" A complete study on how to use "drop 2" chord voicings to create jazz piano magic! 68 pages, plus CD of Mark demonstrating each exercise. $19 list.

"Will make you sound like a real jazz piano player in no time." – Jamey Aebersold

Metaphors For The Musician
By Randy Halberstadt

This practical and enlightening book will help any jazz player or vocalist look at music with "new eyes." Designed for any level of player, on any instrument, "Metaphors For The Musician" provides numerous exercises throughout to help the reader turn these concepts into musical reality.

Guaranteed to help you improve your musicianship. 330 pages – $29 list price. Satisfaction guaranteed!

The Jazz Musicians Guide To Creative Practicing
By David Berkman

Finally a book to help musicians use their practice time wisely! Covers tune analysis, breaking hard tunes into easy components, how to swing better, tricks to playing fast bebop lines, and much more! 150+pages, plus CD. $29 list.

"Fun to read and bursting with things to do and ponder." – Bob Mintzer

The 'Real Easy' Ear Training Book
By Roberta Radley

For all musicians, regardless of instrument or experience, this is the most comprehensive book on "hearing the changes" ever published!

- Covers both beginning and intermediate ear training exercises.
- Music Teachers: You will find this book invaluable in teaching ear training to your students.

Book includes 168 pages of instructional text and musical examples, plus two CDs! $29 list price.

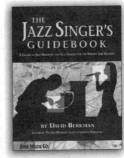

The Jazz Singer's Guidebook By David Berkman
A COURSE IN JAZZ HARMONY AND SCAT SINGING FOR THE SERIOUS JAZZ VOCALIST

A clear, step-by-step approach for serious singers who want to improve their grasp of jazz harmony and gain a deeper understanding of music fundamentals.

This book will change how you hear music and make you a better singer, as well as give you the tools to develop your singing in directions you may not have thought possible.

$26 – includes audio CD demonstrating many exercises.

The Latin Real Book (C, Bb or Eb)

The only professional-level Latin fake book ever published!
Over 570 pages. Detailed transcriptions exactly as recorded by:

Ray Barretto	Arsenio Rodriguez	Manny Oquendo	Ivan Lins
Eddie Palmieri	Tito Rodriguez	Puerto Rico All-Stars	Djavan
Fania All-Stars	Orquesta Aragon	Issac Delgaldo	Tom Jobim
Tito Puente	Beny Moré	Ft. Apache Band	Toninho Horta
Ruben Blades	Cal Tjader	Dave Valentin	Joao Bosco
Los Van Van	Andy Narell	Paquito D'Rivera	Milton Nascimento
NG La Banda	Mario Bauza	Clare Fischer	Leila Pinheiro
Irakere	Dizzy Gilllespie	Chick Corea	Gal Costa
Celia Cruz	Mongo Santamaria	Sergio Mendes	**And Many More!**

The Latin Real Book Sampler CD

12 of the greatest Latin Real Book tunes as played by the original artists: Tito Puente, Ray Barretto, Andy Narell, Puerto Rico Allstars, Bacacoto, etc.

$16 list price. Available in U.S.A. only.

The Conga Drummer's Guidebook By Michael Spiro

Includes CD - $28 list price. The only method book specifically designed for the intermediate to advanced conga drummer. It goes behind the superficial licks and explains how to approach any Afro-Latin rhythm with the right feel, so you can create a groove like the pros!.

"This book is awesome. Michael is completely knowledgable about his subject."
– Dave Garibaldi

"A breakthrough book for all students of the conga drum."
– Karl Perazzo

Introduction to the Conga Drum - DVD
By Michael Spiro

For beginners, or anyone needing a solid foundation in conga drum technique.

Jorge Alabe – "Mike Spiro is a great conga teacher. People can learn real conga technique from this DVD."

John Santos – "A great musician/teacher who's earned his stripes"

1 hour, 55 minutes running time. $25.

Muy Caliente!

Afro-Cuban Play-Along CD and Book
Rebeca Mauleón - Keyboard
Oscar Stagnaro - Bass
Orestes Vilató - Timbales
Carlos Caro - Bongos
Edgardo Cambon - Congas
Over 70 min. of smokin' Latin grooves!
Stereo separation so you can eliminate the bass or piano. Play-along with a rhythm section featuring some of the top Afro-Cuban musicians in the world! $18.

The True Cuban Bass

By **Carlos Del Puerto,** (bassist with Irakere) and **Silvio Vergara**, $22.

For acoustic or electric bass; English and Spanish text; Includes CDs of either historic Cuban recordings or Carlos playing each exercise; Many transcriptions of complete bass parts for tunes in different Cuban styles – the roots of Salsa.

101 Montunos
By Rebeca Mauleón

The only comprehensive study of Latin piano playing ever published.

- Bi-lingual text (English/Spanish)
- 2 CDs of the author demonstrating each montuno
- Covers over 100 years of Afro-Cuban styles, including the danzón, guaracha, mambo, merengue and songo—from Peruchin to Eddie Palmieri. $28

The Salsa Guide Book
By Rebeca Mauleón

The only complete method book on salsa ever published! 260 pages. $25.

Carlos Santana – "A true treasure of knowledge and information about Afro-Cuban music."
Mark Levine, author of The Jazz Piano Book. – "This is the book on salsa."
Sonny Bravo, pianist with Tito Puente – "This will be the salsa 'bible' for years to come."
Oscar Hernández, pianist with Rubén Blades – "An excellent and much needed resource."

The Brazilian Guitar Book
By Nelson Faria, one of Brazil's best new guitarists.

- Over 140 pages of comping patterns, transcriptions and chord melodies for samba, bossa, baião, etc.
- Complete chord voicings written out for each example.
- Comes with a CD of Nelson playing each example.
- The most complete Brazilian guitar method ever published! $28.

Joe Diorio – "Nelson Faria's book is a welcome addition to the guitar literature. I'm sure those who work with this volume will benefit greatly"

Inside The Brazilian Rhythm Section
By Nelson Faria and Cliff Korman

This is the first book/CD package ever published that provides an opportunity for bassists, guitarists, pianists and drummers to interact and play-along with a master Brazilian rhythm section. Perfect for practicing both accompanying and soloing.

$28 list price for book and 2 CDs - including the charts for the CD tracks and sample parts for each instrument, transcribed from the recording.

The Latin Bass Book
A PRACTICAL GUIDE
By Oscar Stagnaro

The only comprehensive book ever published on how to play bass in authentic Afro-Cuban, Brazilian, Caribbean, Latin Jazz & South American styles. $34.

Over 250 pages of transcriptions of Oscar Stagnaro playing each exercise. Learn from the best!

Includes: 3 Play-Along CDs to accompany each exercise, featuring world-class rhythm sections.

Afro-Caribbean Grooves for Drumset

By **Jean-Philippe Fanfant,** drummer with Andy narell's band, Sakesho.

Covers grooves from 10 Caribbean nations, arranged for drumset.

Endorsed by Peter Erskine, Horacio Hernandez, etc.

CD includes both audio and video files. $25.

The Digital Real Book

On the web

Over 850 downloadable tunes from all the Sher Music Co. fakebooks.

See www.shermusic.com for details.

Foundation Exercises for Bass

By Chuck Sher

A creative approach for any style of music, any level, acoustic or electric bass. Perfect for bass teachers!

Filled with hundreds of exercises to help you master scales, chords, rhythms, hand positions, ear training, reading music, sample bass grooves, creating bass lines on common chord progressions, and much more.

$24

Jazz Guitar Voicings The Drop 2 Book

By Randy Vincent, Everything you need to know to create full chord melody voicings like Jim Hall, Joe Pass, etc. Luscious voicings for chord melody playing based on the "Drop 2" principle of chord voicings.

You will find that this book covers this essential material in a unique way unlike any other guitar book available.

Endorsed by Julian Lage, John Stowell, Larry Koonse, etc.

$25, includes 2 CDs.

Walking Bassics: The Fundamentals of Jazz Bass Playing

By swinging NY bassist Ed Fuqua

Includes transcriptions of every bass note on accompanying CD and step-by-step method for constructing solid walking bass lines. $22.

Endorsed by Eddie Gomez, Jimmy Haslip, John Goldsby, etc.

Three-Note Voicings and Beyond

By Randy Vincent, A complete guide to the construction and use of every kind of three-note voicing on guitar.

"Randy Vincent is an extraordinary musician. This book illuminates harmonies in the most sensible and transparent way." – Pat Metheny

"This book is full of essential information for jazz guitarists at any level. Wonderful!" – Mike Stern

194 pages, $28

Concepts for Bass Soloing

By Chuck Sher and Marc Johnson, (bassist with Bill Evans, etc.) The only book ever published that is specifically designed to improve your soloing! $26

• Includes two CDs of Marc Johnson soloing on each exercise
• Transcriptions of bass solos by: Eddie Gomez, John Patitucci, Scott LaFaro, Jimmy Haslip, etc.

"It's a pleasure to encounter a Bass Method so well conceived and executed." – Steve Swallow

The Jazz Piano Book

By Mark Levine, Concord recording artist and pianist with Cal Tjader. For beginning to advanced pianists. The only truly comprehensive method ever published! Over 300 pages. $32

Richie Beirach –"The best new method book available."
Hal Galper – "This is a must!"
Jamey Aebersold – "This is an invaluable resource for any pianist."
James Williams – "One of the most complete anthologies on jazz piano."
Also available in Spanish! ¡El Libro del Jazz Piano!

The Improvisor's Bass Method

By Chuck Sher. A complete method for electric or acoustic bass, plus transcribed solos and bass lines by Mingus, Jaco, Ron Carter, Scott LaFaro, Paul Jackson, Ray Brown, and more! Over 200 pages. $16

International Society of Bassists – "Undoubtedly the finest book of its kind."
Eddie Gomez – "Informative, readily comprehensible and highly imaginative"

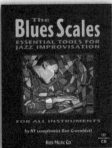

The Blues Scales
ESSENTIAL TOOLS FOR JAZZ IMPROVISATION
By Dan Greenblatt

Great Transcriptions from Miles, Dizzy Gillespie, Lester Young, Oscar Peterson, Dave Sanborn, Michael Brecker and many more, showing how the Blues Scales are actually used in various styles of jazz.

Accompanying CD by author Dan Greenblatt and his swinging quartet of New York jazz musicians shows how each exercise should sound. And it also gives the student numerous play-along tracks to practice with. $22

Essential Grooves
FOR WRITING, PERFORMING AND PRODUCING CONTEMPORARY MUSIC
By 3 Berklee College professors: Dan Moretti, Matthew Nicholl and Oscar Stagnaro

• 41 different rhythm section grooves used in Soul, Rock, Motown, Funk, Hip-hop, Jazz, Afro-Cuban, Brazilian, music and more!
• Includes CD and multi-track DVD with audio files to create play-alongs, loops, original music, and more.

$24

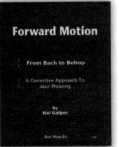

Forward Motion
FROM BACH TO BEBOP
A Corrective Approach to Jazz Phrasing
By Hal Galper

• Perhaps the most important jazz book in a decade, Forward Motion shows the reader how to create jazz phrases that swing with authentic jazz feeling.
• Hal Galper was pianist with Cannonball Adderley, Phil Woods, Stan Getz, Chet Baker, John Scofield, and many other jazz legends.
• Each exercise available on an interactive website so that the reader can change tempos, loop the exercises, transpose them, etc. $30.

The World's Greatest Fake Book

Jazz & Fusion Tunes by: Coltrane, Mingus, Jaco, Chick Corea, Bird, Herbie Hancock, Bill Evans, McCoy, Beirach, Ornette, Wayne Shorter, Zawinul, AND MANY MORE! $32

Chick Corea – "Great for any students of jazz.'
Dave Liebman – "The fake book of the 80's."
George Cables – "The most carefully conceived fake book I've ever seen."